# From
# Learning Disabled
# To

# ENABLED

A mother's journey to find an effective way to teach reading to her daughter and the children she teaches.

## Wendy Crick

Order this book online at www.trafford.com
or email orders@trafford.com

Most Trafford titles are also available at major online book retailers.

Printed in Victoria, BC, Canada.

ISBN: 978-1-4269-0178-2 (sc)
ISBN: 978-1-4269-0907-8 (hc)
ISBN: 978-1-4269-0908-5 (eb)

*Our mission is to efficiently provide the world's finest, most comprehensive book publishing
service, enabling every author to experience success. To find out how to publish your book, your
way, and have it available worldwide, visit us online at www.trafford.com*

*Cover design by Glen McCune*

*Trafford rev. 11/30/09*

 www.trafford.com

**North America & international**
toll-free: 1 888 232 4444 (USA & Canada)
phone: 250 383 6864 ♦ fax: 812 355 4082

To all of the amazing people whom I have met and have yet to meet, who have found their passion and are using it to help others. Also to the countless people who have helped shape this book and to my amazing family: My husband who continues to love and support me even though he does not always understand and my three beautiful children who teach and inspire me to be the best that I can be. Without their tolerance of the computer on during the early morning hours, I would have never been able to complete this book. Thank you.

"The problems of the world cannot possibly be solved by skeptics or cynics…We need men and women who can dream of things that never were."

*John F. Kennedy*

# Preface

This is a story about change and not just a little shift. It's what Phillip Schlechty, in his book *Creating Great Schools*, refers to as "disruptive change". It includes change within a system, but more importantly change within oneself. There is a tidal wave of change that is coming or perhaps is already here. I, along with many others, am leading the way and making the path smoother by lovingly bringing knowledge to those who are seeking it and guiding others who do not yet know what questions to ask.

For me, this course has been frustrating at times, yet more fulfilling than could have been dreamed of. It has led me down many paths that are non-traditional for educators and has given me more knowledge than I ever imagined having. By working my way through the many phases of learning I have discovered great joy, wisdom, and strength. I've ridden this wave for five years and am continually moving forward. Life will never be the same for me and I joyously embrace all that is, has been, and is coming. I have found the answers I was searching for. By writing this book I hope to share those truths and encourage many to start asking questions. In doing so, the transitions between that which has been and that which is here (the paradigm shift) will be easier and smoother.

While the focus of this book is on reading and allowing children to reach their highest potential; there are factors other than lack of reading skills at work which impede children from reaching their highest potential in all subject areas, at all levels. The largest obstacle being: the current structure of our educational system. What many educators do not give much thought to is the fact that we are working within a system (the educational system) that is functionally outdated. The format in which schools operate today has been in place in since the 1920's. Little has changed in the structure of our education system since that time, yet much has changed in our society. "When America's schools were created it was never intended that all students would learn at high levels." (Schlechty 2005). There was an assumption that few students would learn at high levels, many would learn a good deal, some would learn a little, while others would learn simply how to follow directions. The focus was on compliance and attendance rather than successful student engagement. In today's society educators are expected to work within this same system and foster high levels of learning for all. Teachers are held accountable for creating these high levels of learning while using inefficient methods to teach reading. These methods have no intention of allowing all children to reach their highest potential, besides the hindrance of working in a system that does not meet the current expectations of society. This in itself is a major interference for all educators and their students.

Throughout this book I will refer to children who struggle to read. When making this statement, I do not mean that these children have no reading skills, because many have some. My statements come from the perspective that they do not have adequate knowledge and skills to allow them to reach their highest potential, which is what many educators in our society are striving for. As stated previously, this expectation is much different from teaching expectations of the past. If we do not change our methods many more of our students will become a statistic in the ever increasing number of functionally illiterate in America. Without solid, research based reading instruction; thousands more will become a part of the approximately 40 million illiterate or functionally illiterate adults in our country who suffer daily from their lack of reading skills.

Illiteracy can be linked to every socio-economic problem on this planet. There has been much research done, by a variety of different organizations to support this claim. But what can be done about this and how can we cure the illiteracy epidemic which is running rampant across the United States? There are many things that can be done; some are much more time consuming than others. The most immediate and efficient solution is to provide our teachers, parents, and concerned community members with knowledge that is accurate and on the leading edge of scientific research. How do I know? I am a veteran English teacher who has been in the business for twenty years, and like many of my colleagues across this nation, has been searching for more effective ways to teach reading. But it wasn't until my oldest daughter was labeled learning disabled in reading that the quest became personal. Over the past twenty years I have learned and participated in many reading programs with strategies that didn't allow enough children to reach their highest potential. But in knowing what didn't work, I was able to find what did.

After years of searching and learning, I am now aware that there are more efficient and effective ways to teach reading. Ninety five percent of our entire student population can be proficient readers if they are given the right tools. In order to accomplish this lofty task, our teachers must also be given more knowledge and effective strategies. I have been one of the lucky few to discover these truths because of the sheer tenacity of a mother on a mission to save her child regardless of the odds. I have searched for answers as a parent and teacher, and have witnessed the transformation of hundreds into proficient readers with the pure elation and freedom that comes from winning the battle.

By finding ways to help my children and the children I teach, I now have the responsibility to share what I've learned with as many as possible, thus the motivation for this book.

My intention for this book is to bring harmony to a place where there is much discord; in the soul of those who have difficulty reading and to the many educators, parents, and community members searching for a more efficient way to teach reading of the English language. This is a story of my quest to help the world, one child at a time through reading. It tells of the heartache and sorrow along with the triumphs and celebrations.

I love to teach children to read. This is my story......

# Acknowledgments

I would like to very passionately and graciously thank all of the amazing people, including all of my students, who have come into my life and helped me complete this legacy. Some have merely passed through and did or said something inspiring while others have been there guiding me from the very beginning. Of those who deserve special thanks: Ms. Nora Chahbazi and Celeste Hammel. I cannot begin to list all of the ways they have supported me throughout this process. Without Nora and Celeste none of this would have been possible. Thank you to Lynne Zimmer who opened the doors for my daughter and introduced me to Evidence Based Literacy Instruction. Thank you to Amy Dubey, the occupational therapist who chose to help kids above everything else and enlightened me to a whole new realm of the human body and learning. Lastly and perhaps most importantly, my parents; without their teaching and encouragement throughout a life time I would never have had the courage to attempt such a lofty task. May there be blessings galore for each and every person whom has guided me to this point in my life.

# Contents

# Prologue

When embarking on a new adventure, one in which changes your entire way of thinking, believing, and in fact living; there is much to be learned and gained. Although there can be resistance and misunderstanding along this newly chosen path, the wisdom and insight achieved can be unimaginable. This is what has occurred in my life in regards to teaching reading. Never could I have imagined what was set into motion by my daughter Hailey and her struggle to read. Because of my experiences I now know with every part of my being, without the slightest hint of hesitation, that nearly every child in the United States of America can learn how to read, write, and spell at much higher levels. I am talking about every child that has an IQ above 70 being able to perform at or above grade level in reading, writing, and spelling. If teachers, administrators, and interested community leaders knew what many are now learning about the English language and the many aspects that encompass the ability to learn; we could eradicate illiteracy in the United States. Just imagine; a country in which the word illiteracy was hardly ever spoken.

# *1*

# **Where It All Began**

**T**his adventure, like many adventures, began with a damsel in distress, trapped in a tower where no one could reach her. This tower did not have walls visible to the naked eye and she was not trapped by an evil witch. Her captor was the inability to read.

This story began the day my daughter, who was in second grade at the time, came home from school crying—telling me that she couldn't read like the other kids. This cascade of tears and admission was triggered by a fellow student who had declared Hailey was reading "baby books." With Hailey being our first child and me teaching only middle school students, my husband and I didn't really know how her reading compared to other kids. We had no clues previously that there were any problems. She had memorized all of her little practice books sent home from school. She read these books nightly as directed by her teacher. My husband and I, devoted parents, had done all of the things parents were supposed to do to help their children read. We read to her every night, purchased books for her on a regular basis, and were readers ourselves. I was a middle school English teacher for heaven's sake; of course my child could read.

As the year progressed, Hailey had very mysterious stomach problems that only occurred at school. We ended up taking her to several specialists to make sure there truly weren't any physical problems. Nothing physically wrong was found. The doctors attributed the stomach problems to stress and anxiety. As I look back, I realize these symptoms were created from the daily strain of not being able to read.

As she continued to struggle with reading, Hailey was put in a special reading program which incorporated more individualized instruction. Each day for a short period of time she was pulled out of her regular class and worked with an aide on reading in a separate location. Every evening we supported Hailey at home by doing what Hailey's teachers suggested. As Hailey's struggles with reading continued, I realized that none of my college classes had taught me how to teach children to read. I had learned how to administer tests, how to evaluate children's books, and how to create thematic units around books; but nothing on *how* to teach children to read.

We continued with daily pullout sessions and extra practice at home for the rest of second grade. I was frustrated because Hailey was making very little progress and when we read together she would guess at many words. It didn't matter what the word actually was. She would look at the first few letters and guess away at any word she knew that began with these same first few letters. Then she would look up at me with her big brown eyes hoping that her guess was correct. These words, most of the time, made no sense in the context at all. This led to many nights where I would lose my patience and say things like, "How did you get that word? It doesn't have an 's' in it!" I was frustrated and desperate. I asked if our intermediate school district specialist could evaluate her in order for me to acquire more information about what was happening with Hailey. I figured that if we (the teachers and I) could pinpoint some areas of weakness then we could have a better idea as to why she was struggling and how to fix this problem. I was told, "…she may just be developing at a slower rate. Children don't learn at the same rate…. Our district rarely does testing on children before 3rd grade because of their development and you will have to wait until 3rd grade and see because that is where most kids will have everything come together." As I look back, the idea of children developing differently is accurate. Although, in our district (and in many others), all of the teaching children *how* to read was done in grades one and two. By grade three students are expected to have everything in place to be able to read and comprehend text. Most of the reading done in third grade was out of a literature series that offered little in the areas of teaching children *how* to read. So if you didn't "get it" in first or second grades because of developmental reasons, the instruction and opportunities for learning *how* to read in third grade were greatly reduced.

We somehow made it through 2nd grade without too much damage to Hailey's self esteem, although Hailey was under a huge misconception that she was dumb. She knew that she couldn't read like the other kids, even though several people had tried to help her. Hailey thought she was broken and didn't work right. School personnel suggested summer school for additional help. We immediately enrolled Hailey in the summer school program which ran from 8:00 am to 12:00 pm, Monday thru Thursday for the month of June and part of July.

In third grade at the fall parent-teacher conference, I was told Hailey was still struggling with reading. She was not making progress. The teacher also informed me that she thought Hailey had Attention Deficit Disorder (ADD). On top of not being able to read, Hailey would zone out and daydream. I knew that Hailey was not ADD. She could stay on task for long periods, if the tasks did not require reading. In my mind, I thought: I am glad she "zoned out." Zoning out was her way of dealing with the constant bombardment of text that she couldn't read and what she perceived as reinforcement that she was dumb. She was reading at a first grade level while immersed in third grade text and expected to perform at that grade level. In order to keep herself sane she would go to a safer and happier place, a place where she wasn't dumb and wasn't constantly placed in no-win situations. ADD was out of the question. I knew Hailey was smart and could learn to read…. somehow.

The school finally agreed to complete an evaluation. The conclusion they came to was: Hailey was Learning Disabled (LD) in reading. She earned this title because her IQ was average yet her performance on the test was twenty points or more below her ability. With this label, Hailey now qualified for special education services and was given the opportunity to work with a special education teacher to help increase her reading skills. Being a teacher and innately born with the urge to learn, find answers, and solve problems; I wanted more data. I wanted more information on the specific areas of weakness. I also wanted to compare the data. I took Hailey to a local private clinic for evaluation. Several hundred dollars later, I learned that Hailey was dyslexic, and they had specially trained tutors to work with students like Hailey. Everything else they said I did not quite understand. I also found that I could not understand what exactly their tests showed them, nor could I compare the two test batteries. This wasn't because the tests didn't reflect discrepancies; I just wasn't knowledgeable enough to know what to ask or how to interpret the data.

So began the routine of reduced assignments, adaptations such as reading with a peer, group reading, or having someone else read the material to her along with daily special education time where she was still trying to learn how to read. We also opted to have Hailey privately tutored after school with an individual from the dyslexia institute. Hailey worked on reading with her tutor two to three days a week for one hour after school. This was the course of action we followed for the remainder of third grade. As the year progressed, Hailey was making a little progress in reading and she was able to get her daily class work done, although she still wasn't reading at grade level. The year came and went in this way. As summer vacation approached, once again school personnel suggested summer school, so we signed up. We also continued the private tutoring.

Fourth grade was a challenging year. We continued with Hailey getting private tutoring after school, although she still was not making significant progress in reading. She was now in 4th grade with a 2nd grade reading level. Hailey's work load increased and she had hours of homework each night just to keep up with daily assignments. Hailey continued to convince herself that she was dumb. She created many ways to hide her "disability". The trick she used most often was pretending to read. She would check out books from the library that were well above her ability level and pretend to read them. For class assignments she would pretend to read while carefully listening to others in order to write some answers on her paper. Her teachers were fantastic with helping her accept herself as she was and not allowing her to wallow in self pity. They helped her create ways in which to compensate for her inability to read while allowing her to shine in other areas where she excelled. As the year progressed she actually began to like herself and be more accepting of her uniqueness.

As spring parent-teacher conferences grew closer, I looked forward to hearing what kind of progress Hailey had made in reading. I sat down and could never have imagined what was about to be said. With tears rolling down my face I heard that Hailey had made very little progress and that she "would probably never be able to read past the 4th grade level; her brain was just wired differently". I was also told that her math was very low and she could possibly qualify for special education in math.

My heart was breaking. How could this happen? My husband and I had done everything we possibly could with tutoring, practicing reading every night, and supporting Hailey to complete all of her class work. Hailey had given everything that she had and still there was such little progress. I remember saying, "You mean to tell me that when Hailey is an adult she will not be able to pick up a horse magazine and read about her one passion in life? What about college and a career?" Hailey had the personality and people skills to create opportunities, but I wanted her to have the skills necessary to be able to follow her dreams, wherever they may lead. I walked out of that meeting broken. I was absolutely at a loss. I felt powerless and hopeless. I had no answers. I had no knowledge of how to fix things. How could I protect my little princess from the hardships that would follow? How could I have failed my child?

We stopped the tutoring and did not attend summer school that summer. For a few months a darkness surrounded me, and I mourned the loss of opportunities for our daughter because of her inability to read beyond a third grade level. And for a short period of time I accepted the fallacy that Hailey could not learn how to read. I accepted it so completely; I even went as far as contacting the local library for the blind in order to get all of Hailey's textbooks and classroom novels recorded on tape for the upcoming school year. I thought at least this way she could more easily keep up with her studies and her peers.

Then came the days when I started to question. Why was it that Hailey could not read? With all of the amazing and intelligent people in this world, why was it that we as educators could not teach some children to read? I began to think back on my 16 years of teaching and of the students who had entered my 6th grade classroom not able to read at grade level. I thought of the kids whom I had worked with to try and bring up their reading skills and the parents who had come to me and asked if I could teach their child to read because they were still struggling with reading in 6th grade. I came to the realization of two very important things. *1. I did not know how to teach kids to read. 2. It was not the kids: it was the system that was broken.*

# 2

# Grab Your Bootstraps and Let's Get To Work!

Hailey continued in fifth grade with the label of LD in reading. Although she would possibly "qualify" in math, I would not allow her to be labeled LD in math also. She was barely hanging on emotionally and I was not about to have her completely give up on herself with the idea that she also couldn't achieve in math. I started looking for any reading programs that were different. We had at this point tried three different "reading programs"—none had given Hailey the knowledge she needed to succeed in reading. Meanwhile, Hailey learned to work in groups with peers or with books on tape and she stayed after school for extra math help. Her teachers were all very supportive and enjoyed having Hailey in class, but no one had the answers I was seeking. She also continued to be pulled out for special reading help. Everyone was doing the best they could, but they were all under the same misconception: Hailey would never be a reader.

I spoke with fellow colleagues, specialists at our intermediate school district, and attended numerous conferences on reading. I found that most programs looked very similar to what we had already tried and that if a teacher and a student worked hard, the student might get one year's growth out of one year's worth of work. Many teachers and administrators were happy with that progress. That expectation was not acceptable to me; one year of growth for one year of work would never catch Hailey, and other kids like her, up to grade level. I needed something that could get her back on track quickly. I was amazed at how hard kids, like Hailey, would work in 5th, 6th, and 7th grade to continually try to learn how to read. Many still had the faith and hope to try. I knew that if we didn't find the answers in middle school they would be lost. They would give up, possibly drop out of school, and many opportunities would not be available to them as adults. I was frustrated, angry, and burned out. I thought of a job change. Perhaps there were other ways in which I could help children. Maybe there were no answers that I could find? So I prayed. I prayed that I could find help for Hailey. And I prayed that God would show me answers and help me find where I belonged. I knew that I belonged in teaching somewhere, but I wasn't sure where anymore.

Fifth grade continued with difficulty. Hailey was doing fairly well in school. She had a lot of friends, was involved with extra curricular activities, and received average grades. Evenings and homework were Hell at our house. Hailey and I would fight because she wasn't focusing on her work. I didn't think that she was actually trying to read because she persistently guessed at words.

Her spelling was also horrendous. Each marking period she was upset because she did not get on the honor roll. Her grades were never quite good enough to make the list because of her reading disability. This really upset her since all of her friends were on the honor roll and had special signs on their lockers along with their names being listed in the school newsletter. I just kept telling her that it would be alright, that she was good at other things, like horseback riding, and other kids weren't. She told me no one got to see her be good at those things like everyone did with reading and the honor roll. She was right.

In the spring, my daughters and I were at a horse show and I ran into an old friend and teacher, Lynne Zimmer, who I hadn't seen in at least ten years. Lynne told me about some new reading strategies she had been trained in and how she was using them with great success. She was privately tutoring students in the area and gave me a pamphlet. She said if I knew anyone who needed help to give them her name. I said sure, put the pamphlet in my bag, and continued to catch up on old news. We enjoyed the horse show and went our separate ways. At the time I didn't really think of the possibility of Hailey working with her because I had bought into the myth that Hailey "was wired differently" and would never be a good reader.

Hailey's fifth grade year was coming to an end quickly and before we knew it, summer vacation was here. Hailey was happy to be free of class work and be able to ride her horse. I was concerned because she was going to be entering middle school and I knew first hand the work load she would be encountering there. The name Lynne Zimmer popped into my head. Yes, Lynne had said that she had some amazing strategies. We had lain off tutoring for one year and it was now summer vacation. I thought: Well we have nothing to lose; let's try this one last thing. If this doesn't work, I will give up and accept the fact that Hailey and other kids are just wired differently and they will never be good readers. Lynne was called, I found out a little more about the Evidence Based Literacy Instruction (EBLI) strategies she was using, and set up a tutoring schedule. EBLI was different. The tutoring and teaching of the strategies had an approximate time line. There were a set amount of sessions that Lynne would work with Hailey, and that was it. Wow, everything else we had experienced or looked into did not have this set amount of time for the average student to learn. With other programs, one just seemed to tutor forever with no end. Hailey, not as enthused as I, reluctantly agreed to be tutored.

Lynne began in late June and came to our home three times a week at 9:00 a.m. Hailey, a typical I-WANT-TO-SLEEP-TILL-NOON middle school kid, did not like getting out of bed let alone working on reading. Oppositional defiant was a good term to describe Hailey. She *hated* reading and felt it was dumb. She was there because I was making her. She did not believe it would make any difference. I watched. This was a different approach than anything I had seen. I liked it and hoped it would work. Hailey continued to be tutored throughout the months of July and August with some time off here and there for vacations and horse shows. She was making progress! She was not guessing at words nearly as much and she could read multi-syllable words, although it was still very slow and difficult for her. After just a few weeks Hailey was reading at a fourth grade level and could decode words at a sixth grade level. I was ecstatic. Hailey thought it was okay, but still wasn't convinced. Lynne was happy but wanted to keep going with Hailey. She thought Hailey had some processing issues going on and that the flood gates would open up at any time. It was now the end of August and Hailey had worked with Lynn for approximately six weeks (about18, one hour sessions). School began and Lynne was able to come to our middle school and work with her one hour a week. Lynne and I were not giving up on Hailey. She still had to reach that 6th grade reading level which meant she needed to be reading 140 words per minute, in 6th grade text and comprehend what she read in order to be on track.

In October Hailey came into my classroom after a tutoring session with Lynne. She was very excited because she had just gone to the library and found a book that she really liked and enjoyed reading. She had found *The Lion, the Witch and the Wardrobe.*

# 3

# Fall, Floodgates, and Narnia

I will never forget that day! My emotions were running rampant. I wanted to yell, scream with joy, and cry all at the same time. Because I couldn't do all of those things in front of my students and embarrass Hailey, I simply said, "Great job Hailey, I knew you could do it!" After school I sat alone in my classroom and cried. They were tears of joy, and I thanked God for Lynne Zimmer, EBLI, and the divine intervention that had brought us all together.

From that day forward my husband and I could not get Hailey to put books down. She began with the magic of Narnia and continued on to many other books and magazines. She was starving for information and couldn't read enough. Every night as I walked passed her bedroom she would be reading. For many months, tears would come to my eyes as I watched her read. She especially loved books on history. I remember taking her to a book store and she asked me where she could find books on the Great Depression and the Vietnam War. We began to have discussions about books and history. What a wonderful gift she had been given!

That year was the first year Hailey earned high enough grades to get on the honor roll. And that little piece of paper on her locker that she had longed for? It was there for everyone to see! Hailey Crick had done it: She had beaten the odds and learned how to read! We celebrated! An eternal flame was ignited, one which continues to burn brightly today. I could hardly believe she was the same child. Actually she wasn't the same child. She was now the Hailey she was born to be: intelligent, vibrant, and enthusiastic about life.

Hailey continued on through seventh and eighth grade with all A's, earning her spot on the superintendent's list. She was still legally a special education student with the LD label, although she did not use any of the special education services. In the spring of her freshman year at high school, Hailey was tested by our intermediate school district's reading specialist to see if she still qualified for special education services. Hailey scored at a twelfth grade comprehension level and was a fluent reader. Her writing was also above grade level. She was officially booted out of special education and left the label of learning disabled (LD) behind! Today, she is taking honors level classes in math, science, history, and English with a B+ average and has big plans for her future.

.........And so this story ends with the princess being rescued from her tower. Although, she was not rescued by a handsome prince, simply a mom who was stubborn enough and strong enough to battle the dragons and save her princess. The handsome prince? That story has yet to be written.

# 4

# The Adventure Continues

After the amazing transformation witnessed in my daughter, there was a deep calling for me: a life's mission. Moved by the progress Hailey made and seeing the difference Evidence Based Literacy Instruction (EBLI) had on her life; I needed to do something about it. Others needed to learn what we had experienced. I now had a purpose and a path to follow.

My first step into the mayhem of reading reform began at the dealership waiting for my car to be repaired. I'd just spoken to my friend Lynne who had tutored Hailey. She had recently returned from an updated training in Evidence Based Literacy Instruction. She was excited about the new information shared and commented on how she learned 80% more at this training than she knew while tutoring Hailey. I was amazed. I needed to do something. I felt the strong need to take action and begin making a difference in other children's lives. I asked Lynne, "What's the bottom line? How much is this going to cost me? I have to get trained." Lynne replied, "One thousand dollars."

As our conversation ended I was left wondering where I was going to get one thousand dollars. My principal was supportive, but wanted more information and wasn't sure if we had the money in our budget. Sure there was money in my checking, but it was already set aside for bills. So I did the next best thing, pulled out what I call a girl's best friend…*PLASTIC*. Never in my life had I used a credit card for this large of a purchase and especially not without discussing it with my husband. The next thing I knew my cell phone was ringing and Ounce of Prevention Reading Center in Flushing, Michigan was on the other end. They took plastic! At the time, I had no idea where this adventure would lead: I knew I just needed to do it.

My drive home was euphoric. Who knew how long it was going to take me to pay off the credit card, but it was what had to be done. I felt elated and free: The freedom that comes with knowing you have just done something that is absolutely correct and in perfect harmony with your next great adventure. There was still one little nagging detail; how to break the news to my husband.

It took a few days before there was an appropriate time to tell my husband. The funny thing was I never did actually tell him the cost. I remember sitting in our great room telling him about Lynne and the new things that she had learned. He was mildly interested, nodding his head politely as he read a magazine. I then explained about wanting to get the training. He asked, "Why?" I simply replied, "To help other children." He then asked, "How much will it cost?" My response was, "How can we put a price tag on what we have seen and experienced? Think of the many children I work with and their parents. I have the opportunity to help others who don't know where to turn and believe that their child will never be able to read. What a priceless gift." That was the end of our conversation. He never asked the bottom line and it didn't matter because our lives would never be the same!

A few weeks later, the adventure truly began. Never would I have imagined what began as a nightmare with no foreseeable answers for our family would lead me to all of the knowledge, wisdom, and amazing experiences I've had since my training. Without a doubt the training was the best use of one thousand dollars I have ever spent!

The Evidenced Based Literacy Instruction training was life altering. Everything fit together. The examples, strategies, data, and reasoning all made perfect sense to me; they were the answers I had been searching for. Divine intervention had given me the most perfect gift; I was ready to accept it and practice the strategies in order to help kids. After arriving home from the training, I went right to work. My two nieces, who were having troubles with reading and school work, became my guinea pigs. We worked for two months, twice a week during the summer. I wasn't quite sure if any of this new information was making a difference or if I was doing it right. Time would tell.

While tutoring my nieces, I shared with my principal what I had done and where we could go with it. He was surprised, to say the least. When he told me he wasn't sure if we had money in the budget; he assumed I would just wait on the training. Ah, but not me, a woman on her path of destiny! Since first mentioning the training we hadn't spoken because he had gotten married and had been on his honeymoon. He had no idea that I had gone ahead with the training. Now I was trained and wanted to integrate the new reading strategies into my classes! My principal wanted to support me in whatever ways he could and we immediately set to work. We were able to do some creative scheduling and persuade two additional teachers to assist in a reading class that used the EBLI strategies. We were also able to get some local grant money to help offset part of my training costs and purchase some additional materials.

As the school year began I learned that my nieces were excelling in reading and their grades in all of their classes had come up significantly since the EBLI tutoring. We, the two other teachers and I, had also begun using the reading strategies in a classroom within both large and small group settings. After two months of teaching reading using the EBLI strategies, we were astonished. We had middle school kids that entered our class between 2nd and 4th grade reading levels move two to four grade levels in two months! **Yes, I said that right: two to four grade levels in just two months!** It was the most joyful and fulfilling experience I had ever had in teaching! Kids were happy, parents were overjoyed, and my principal was impressed.

We were moving kids in and out of that reading class like an assembly line. We would do some prescreening to diagnose their weakness and prescribe what they needed to get back on track. Working in small groups and rotating through centers, we were able to get most kids beyond grade level and out into their regular reading class in a matter of weeks or months. It was fun! The skills I had learned allowed me to diagnose each child's problem and prescribe the strategies needed to fix the problem. Some of the students we had were special education students with learning disability labels or cognitive impairments; others were regular education students struggling with fluency and comprehension. It was and still is simply remarkable to me. Sometimes when we worked with kids, we only needed a few hours and they were on track and on their way. An extra bonus of using the EBLI strategies was we also saw a marked improvement in spelling and writing along with the reading. Without a doubt the Evidence Based Literacy Instruction strategies were the most effective and efficient ways I'd found to teach people how to read the English language. The reason these strategies worked so well was the fact that they were created from knowledge of how the brain synthesizes and organizes information, an understanding that our language is created by phonemes (units of sound) that are represented by graphemes (letters), and the most common spelling tendencies of the sounds that appear in the English language. Also included were strategies in segmenting and blending along with fluency training and vocabulary building. Theses strategies in conjunction with the sequence of instruction and dialogue produced amazing results in a short period of time.

As I shared these results with colleagues I was met with a variety of responses. Some were very excited and wanted to learn the strategies themselves. In fact, twenty teachers from five different school districts joined my classroom to observe what we did and how it was implemented during our first year of using the

EBLI strategies. Although there were others who were skeptical and did not believe we were actually getting the results reported. Sadly, there were also others who were afraid or resentful. They felt their way of teaching reading was being attacked and did not understand that these strategies could only enhance what they were currently doing. None of them had experienced what I had and did not understand why I was searching for something that was more efficient. Because of my experiences, I knew first hand that a much higher percentage of children could be proficient readers. I wanted, then and now, to help *all* children achieve their highest potential by giving them the tools and knowledge to be amazing readers.

Many skeptics wanted data: cold hard evidence to support my claims. For me, data wasn't necessary—I had lived it— but I understood their need. This led me to another road, one of research and data, which I am very thankful for. This forced me to understand fully why EBLI is so powerful and know what sets the EBLI strategies apart from so many other strategies being practiced today.

# 5

# The Brain, It's Processing, and Teaching

**B**efore we discuss what have been or still are the most commonly used practices to teach reading today in the United States, we must first have an understanding of how the brain organizes information and stores it into long term memory, which is what learning truly is.

Humans are perceptual learners. In simplified terms this means: we take in information from our environment through our senses and process that information into categories or groups by looking for common patterns or tendencies so that it can be stored in long term memory. After a pattern is stored, the human can then recognize a pattern and add to it as their experiences and exposure to new information increases. For school aged children and adults, the most commonly used skills are the visual perceptual skills and the auditory perceptual skills. In other words, when we as learners come across some new piece of information or knowledge we look at it very carefully to see any patterns or common tendencies or we listen very carefully for the details so we can connect this new knowledge with some pre-existing pattern we have stored in long term memory. Sometimes we must also rely on our tactile sense, but not nearly as often as our visual and auditory. If you look at schools today, the majority of teaching is visual and auditory as opposed to tactile (hands on). We see more tactile learning incorporated within the pre-school and lower elementary teaching than anywhere else. And that is where most should be. (Rosner, 1979) Typically educators know the enhanced learning power of incorporating an element of the tactile into teaching new lessons and do so at many grade levels when introducing a new concept. When the opportunity arises to use ones visual, auditory, and tactile to learn new information the retention of that learning is much higher.

As we delve into the subject of reading programs typical in education today, I want you to think about one last bit of information connected to perceptual learning and teaching. Let's quickly look at how core subjects, other than reading, in our education system are taught. History:  When teaching this subject much information is grouped together by time lines or ages. Each time in history is grouped together by common traits or characteristics. These common traits or characteristics are then intentionally and systematically taught. The information given is connected to pre-learned concepts and builds. As the learner progresses, he or she is then able to use the stored information to make inferences about historical events. In science the different branches are grouped together by common characteristics, biology, sociology, psychology…. Even within some of these subjects areas there are groupings; for example in Biology there are kingdom, phylum and class used to categorize living organisms. In each of these, details and facts are systematically taught. The information taught is constantly connected to patterns previously housed in the brain. In math everything is based on patterns and groupings. These patterns are continually added to and built upon throughout a student's educational career. Now, what about reading? ***Do we teach the code (patterns) of the English language in a systematic and intentional way? Do we use the knowledge of how the brain organizes information and apply it to learning one of the most complex languages in the world?***

Here are a couple of analogies that may help paint a clearer picture of what I am alluding to. When teaching multiplication tables in math, the teacher intentionally and systematically teaches all of the times tables, usually 0 thru 12. They do not teach only the 1's, 3's, 5,' and 7's and expect the students to see the pattern and catch on to it. They do this because they know this knowledge is the building blocks of concepts to come. In history we do not give kids random dates with general information and expect them to just figure out what occurred. Nor do history teachers teach his or her students, this time period was considered the roaring 20's, then came The Great Depression, and expect the students to figure out what happened and why on their own. These teachers intentionally and systematically teach the characteristics so that a student can refer back to their previously learned information (pattern) and apply it while adding new information to the patterns already acquired. Yet, in the teaching of reading many educators do not teach all of the code of the English language. For example the spelling "ch", children are intentionally taught the "ch" represents the sound /ch/ as in <u>ch</u>ur<u>ch</u> or crun<u>ch</u>. Sometimes students may intentionally be taught that the letters "ch" can also represent the sound /k/ as in <u>Ch</u>ristmas. Although I have found many students who can read and spell Christmas because they have seen it in print so often, yet cannot transfer the knowledge of the "ch" representing /k/ when reading or spelling the word me<u>ch</u>anic. Not many educators today intentionally teach that "ch" can also represent the /sh/ sound as in ma<u>ch</u>ine or <u>ch</u>ute. If a student were systematically and intentionally taught that the letters "ch" can represent different sounds then they could see the pattern, store this information in long term memory, and use it in decoding other words they encounter with the "ch" spelling.

This is what is meant by "teaching all of the code". This example of teaching the *code* of the English language is effective because of the way the human brain stores and retrieves information. Why don't teachers use this systematic and logical sequence of instruction? Most teachers have not been taught or shown all of the patterns that exist within our alphabetical writing system. This filtration of the most recent and intensive research about teaching reading done in the scientific community has also been very slow, to say the least, to diffuse into the educational community.

Many teachers across the United States still cling to the concept of teaching words as a whole. When teachers use this strategy what pattern do children have to connect to? Is there any pattern in a list of words that are posted on the wall and must be memorized? If this works then why do so many children still have trouble reading and spelling these "sight words or word wall words" in the upper grades?

Many will argue that we have a majority of students who learn how to read despite the non linear methods used. This is true, although are those students reading at their highest potential or are they simply near grade level? Are they able to keep up as multi-syllable words are introduced? How is their spelling? Do they understand the patterns of our language to spell correctly? And why wouldn't you teach this challenging language systematically and logically?

Whether the educational community consistently teaches the patterns within our language or not kids will create their own patterns in order to learn the language. Sometimes a student will pick up on accurate patterns that can be applied consistently throughout our language in order to be a proficient reader and speller; although most of the time the patterns that students pick up on are nonsensical and will only work a fraction of the time within our language. If you don't believe me, just sit down with a student who struggles with reading or spelling and ask them why they read or spelled the word in that way. I guarantee; you will be very surprised by the answers you receive.

Keep these questions and statements in mind as you read about the history of teaching reading.

# 6

# History of Reading:
# A Cliff Notes Version

## *Phonics*

T he idea of teaching everyone how to read began with Martin Luther in the 17th century. Martin Luther, the creator of the Lutheran Church, and his followers were the inventors of phonics. Luther split from the Catholic Church because of his feelings that all people should be able to read the bible, not in Latin, but in their own language. He and his followers began by translating the bible and other important scripture into English. This led him to create a way to teach the masses to read since most people during this time period could not read. He created the method of phonics. This method was based on the knowledge that English consists of an alphabetic writing system. In an alphabetic system, symbols (letters) are used to represent sounds. Luther taught the 44 sounds of the English language which included knowledge of the overlap of sounds in the alphabetic code, for example /k/ can be "c"or "k". The teaching of phonics at this stage consisted of mostly alphabetic code training, syllable memorization, and decoding words by sounding them out. When learners had progressed to the point where they could identify single words, they were given simple sentences to read. Naturally, this progressed to the point where they were reading regular text from books. This system of teaching reading continued for the next 200 years.

During the 19th century the system was changed slightly by adding diagraphs and rules. Diagraphs are the two letter combinations in the English language that represent one sound such as "ch", "th", and "sh". Learning phonics with the rules was a laborious job and required even more memorization. Today many still use this method or parts of it to teach reading.

There have been several criticisms of phonics that still exist today. The most significant complaint is that there is too much "drill and kill". In other words, children are given a lot of worksheets where they learn words and rules, yet they do not spend enough time in text. Another complaint is that children taught only using phonics can read a word properly yet may still have no idea of what the word means. Many educators have also found that learning all of the rules is difficult and that these rules are not accurate 30% to 40 % of the time. One example of this is the commonly taught rule, "two vowels go walking and the first does the talking". This rule is true some of the time but not all. Here are just a few words that don't follow the rule: steak, boil, out, you, again, tough, fruit, taught, mountain… and the list can go on. Another example of a very confusing rule for anyone learning to read English is the idea of silent letters. Letters do not have voices and they do not talk. They are just symbols that represent a sound. Children taught "silent letters" have a very difficult time with words like "laugh" because they may have been told that the "gh" is silent as in the word "light". Students also have a difficult time deciding when a letter should be "silent" and when it shouldn't.

Another problem for teachers is the lack of understanding and knowledge of what phonics truly is. The clearest definition of phonics I've discovered is: a method of teaching reading in which people learn to associate letters with the speech sounds they represent, rather than learning to recognize the whole word as a unit. In order to be proficient at teaching phonics a teacher must have an understanding of phonology and orthography, but there are few courses that adequately address these subjects in colleges and universities around the United States. Without this knowledge even those teachers using a phonetic approach have fallen short. Their students do not know enough of the code to reach their highest potential in reading *and* spelling. Many teachers coming out of our universities say they have the big picture. They know about literature, how to evaluate it, and create thematic units, but they don't have a clue about how to actually teach reading—phonics, decoding, fluency, and comprehension.

Because of these downfalls with the phonics approach, many educators have discontinued the use in their classrooms which has led to a large number of students not proficient in reading or spelling.

## *Basal Readers*

The next phase of teaching reading came in the 1860's with the creation of basal readers. This began with a series called the McGuffey Reader. Later came the more well know basal readers *Dick and Jane* or *Spot the Dog* books. They were the first books published for schools with the idea of having one text for each grade level. These books emphasized memorizing words by sight, which became known as the "look and say" method. Today it may be referred to as the "whole word" approach. Basal readers were published with the idea of teaching reading in a more organized way. Each book was a collection of short stories especially written for young readers. One characteristic of these books was the stories all contained a few words or phrases which were continually repeated throughout the story. These words and phrases were pre-taught to the class. This was called a controlled vocabulary and students practiced the "look and say" method. The practice was to memorize each word needed to read the new story. In this way, the class learned to read. As the class progressed, the number of words taught to the class increased as well. There was also some modified "phonic" alphabet teaching included in this series such as "ch", "th", and "sh". The vocabulary and phonics skills were taught in consumable books called "workbooks". This method worked especially well if a student had a good memory. It was also very teacher friendly. For many teachers who did not have adequate training in reading, this was very helpful. The teacher was able to open the teacher's manual and the lessons were written out, along with dialog to follow. The workbooks allowed the students to practice phonics skills while the teacher had time to read with smaller groups. This method of teaching reading became immediately popular and still continues to be popular in many parts of the United States.

Critics of this system feel that it also has several shortcomings. The most prevalent complaint is that all or most of the words learned by students are memorized words instead of learning to decode words phonetically. This memorization method works for children with good memories although even children with excellent memories have trouble remembering after a few years (usually second or third grade) because of memory overload. Once the student is introduced to multi-syllable words the sheer number of words needed to be memorized increases dramatically. Just like the hard drive on a computer runs out of space, our memories fill up too. Signs of memory overload are commonly seen when children confuse words like "quit, quiet, and quite", "were and where" or "through and though". They look visually similar and since the child has no other strategies to help distinguish between them they are often confused.

Another criticism of basal readers is when multi-syllable words are introduced outside the basal reader's controlled vocabulary many students have trouble decoding the words. The main strategies taught in the basal readers for decoding multi-syllable words is to look for smaller words within larger words or to look at the first sound and the ending sound in a word and guess what the word is based on the context. Both of these strategies are not efficient. The method of looking for smaller words within multi-syllable words does work for some words (usually compound words) but not most.

One example of this is the word "conscience". Using this method most children would see "con" and "science" and are not able to make the leap to "conscience" because of the lack of practice in decoding a word sound by sound and knowledge of the code of the English language. For this word a student would need to know that "sc" can be a spelling for /sh/ and "ie" is a spelling for /ĕ/.

Two other criticisms of the basal reader are over how the reading skills and spelling are taught. The reading skills are taught in isolation and spelling is taught by memorization. It is felt by many that teaching skills in isolation can be learned by students. This is one thought process; another is applying that skill in text. Some feel students are not taught how to apply the skills in text through the basal readers. As far as memorizing spelling words, the argument goes back to the inability to memorize every word in English. Teachers and parents alike have witnessed time and time again students who memorize their spelling words before a test, take the test, and do not remember how to spell the words by the next day or even the next hour.

Rudolph Flesch became one of the most outspoken and well known opponents of basal readers when he published *Why Johnny Can't Read* in 1950. He argued that there were two significant problems with basal readers: 1) they were "essentially dull and meaningless texts that failed to engage children in a desire to read." 2) They were "responsible for creating reading disabilities because they failed to provide children with opportunities to learn the phonemic skills needed to become independent, self-guided readers" (Mitchell and Boyd 2001). This began the movement to use methods referred to as "whole language".

## *Whole Language*

The whole language approach represents a philosophy about reading and language development rather than an instructional method. In the 1980's this movement gained wide spread support from thousands of teachers. According to this philosophy, language is an innate phenomenon that children learn naturally; therefore reading can be learned effortlessly. With this method, the teacher has a "big book", which is an actual book big enough for the class to see and read along with the teacher. The teacher reads the "big book" with the class, and then the students can reread the book in a smaller version with friends, family, or alone. The theory behind this method is that children will automatically assimilate the skills that are necessary to read without the need to learn phonics because it is presented in authentic text. Authentic text is considered a book rich in language, that is not limited by a restricted vocabulary.

One of the reading strategies taught by whole language teachers for identifying unknown words is the cloze strategy. Cloze strategy consists of skipping the word, reading the words around the unknown word, using context clues to figure out what the word is, and hoping you guess the correct word for the unknown word. Once again, we see the adoption of guessing as a reading strategy. This is not an effective strategy and does not teach accuracy. There are too many words in the English language that may fit. Another strategy taught is to look at the pictures and try to guess what the word might be. We have all heard the old cliché: a picture is worth a thousand words. Also, why teach a strategy that *may* work if the student guesses the correct word for the picture, although will be worthless once they progress out of picture books?

Whole Language also uses the strategy of using initial consonants. Here's an example of this strategy: If a child is trying to decode the word *porch,* the first thing he would do is to skip the· word. For example, the teacher would read aloud to him," Frog and Toad sat on the 'blank', feeling sad together." The child would then look at the picture and say something like, "stoop". Next he may say, "No, it can't be stoop, it doesn't start with's'; it's a 'p'". The teacher then reads the sentence again and the child says "porch" (Raines, 1995). Hopefully the child will say porch and not "patio" or "place" or a variety of other words beginning with the letter "p" that would fit in this context. Many feel this internal dialog that the reader is engaged in distracts the reader and impedes comprehension. Another criticism of these methods is there's too much room for error. With the cloze method and the method that focuses on only the beginning consonant, students can choose a variety of different words that may fit. The method of using the picture to guess the word is not efficient either. None of these strategies teach accuracy. Good readers read with near perfect accuracy.

Along with whole language came "inventive spelling". The idea behind inventive spelling was that children could spell words like they sounded. It was felt that using this method wouldn't destroy the spontaneity of writing. Children could write without having to stop and learn the correct spelling of a word.

The main criticism with inventive spelling is that by allowing children to consistently write words incorrectly they are learning and constantly seeing the incorrect spelling which leads to incorrect knowledge of the code of the English language. This inaccuracy then leads to problems with decoding words. Allowing inventive spelling also creates the problem of trying to re-teach children, at some point in their educational career, the correct spelling of words.

Phonics, Basal Readers, and Whole Language have been the most commonly used methods to teach reading over the past 200 years. Currently many schools may use a more eclectic approach, sometimes referred to as a "balanced approach" or "balanced literacy", where they use bits and pieces of each of these methods when teaching children to read. Whether a balanced approach or not, according to research, many programs that are commonly used in America today come up short. On average 30 to 40 percent of fourth grade students do not achieve the skills needed to be proficient readers throughout adulthood. Standardized test scores across the nation reflect this trend. Data from the National Assessment of Educational Progress (NAEP) 1992 Reading Report Card shows that the highest scoring state had 29 percent of all students below basic level reading skills and the bottom states doubled this rate with the lowest state score of 75 percent of students below basic reading skills. And those numbers are most likely lower since this data does not include special education students with IEP's (Individual Education Plans) or students with limited English proficiency. The results for the adult population were not much better, reflecting that forty-two million adults are functionally illiterate (McGuinness, 1997). This data, along with the trends that I have seen in my classroom over the past 20 years, and Hailey's experiences have led me to find something more effective and efficient.

Before I share with you what I have found you must have an understanding of why it works by gaining a better knowledge of our writing system. Our writing system is an alphabetic system, which means that we have arbitrary symbols that represent sounds. It is a code. It is also opaque, meaning obscure and unclear in meaning. In plain English this means: the random letters put together have no meaning until we give them meaning. We must attach meaning to the symbols or letters. In order for anyone to teach children how to read English they must have a broad knowledge of the sounds (phonemes) that make up our system and the symbols (letters or graphemes) which we use to represent those sounds. Yep, that means exactly what you are thinking: Phonemic awareness and phonics must be taught. *Once again, as I speak of phonics I am referring to a method of teaching reading in which people learn to associate letters with the speech sounds they represent, rather than learning to recognize the whole word as a unit.*

With the recent release of what is considered the largest and most in depth study of reading to date, the National Reading Panel's findings clearly reflect that every program producing the highest rate of success included some type of phonics instruction. A summary of the *U.S. National Reading Panel Report Teaching Children to Read* prepared by the Division of Research and Policy,

International Reading Association, stated: " The panel determined that effective reading instruction includes teaching children to break apart and manipulate the sounds in words (phonemic awareness), teaching them that these sounds are represented by letters that can be blended together to form words (phonics), having them practice what they've learned by reading aloud with guidance and feedback ( guided oral reading), and teaching them to apply strategies to guide and improve reading comprehension." Another interesting find in the National Reading Panel's research is that the panel examined 35 years of research, which included 40 thousand programs, and of those programs less than one thousand were considered usable because the data was not valid and/or reliable. This information seems to further validate why many reading programs used in our schools today aren't producing enough proficient readers.

The National Institutes of Health also conducted a study on reading which included this statement: "A major finding stated in the report is that the poorest readers used context clues to figure out words while the best readers decoded the "sounds" made by the letters." They further stated, 'The ability to process sounds that are heard (called phonological processing) consistently differentiates good readers and poor readers,'" (America Reads Challenge National Institute of Child Health and Human Development Research).

When discussing phonics, many veteran educators who have taught reading for years and have lived through a variety of trends know from experience that including phonics in their teaching has yielded better readers. However, many educators are frustrated because in their opinion, the use of phonics is still not getting all of their children up to levels that are necessary for proficiency and life long success. The reason for this frustration is most educators have not been given accurate or thorough knowledge about our alphabetic writing system and the common spelling tendencies in the English language. Our universities and colleges training our teachers offer few courses on phonology (the study of speech sounds in our language) and orthography (the study of letters of an alphabet and how they occur sequentially in words). Most teachers in our schools today do not realize the English language is made up of approximately 44 different sounds and that those sounds can be represented by approximately 100 different letter combinations. Many teachers are only teaching part of the code in a chaotic, nonsensical way along with very little decoding skills. This trend is what has led me to Evidenced Based Literacy Instruction. I would also be in support of any other reading programs that elicited explicit instruction in the depth and scope of our writing system, incorporated strategies based on brain research, as well as comprehensive reading data. However, as of this writing I have yet to find any as comprehensive and efficient as Evidence Based Literacy Instruction.

# 7

# What is EBLI?

Evidence Based Literacy Instruction (EBLI) is a set of strategies that is used to teach knowledge of the English language and accuracy in reading and spelling. The strategies allow readers to have a clear and systematic understanding of how our language is put together which allows *all* readers to achieve at their highest potential. The strategies are based on the English phonemic writing system, understanding the spelling code of the English language, and how the brain organizes information. These strategies teach that our language is made up of sounds that are represented by symbols (letters). Good readers must be able separate the individual sounds and know the symbols that spell these sounds. Readers must also be able to segment and blend sounds and understand that our language has a variety of spellings for the same sound. The EBLI strategies systematically teach what readers need to know and integrate in order to comprehend the English language.

These strategies have been created by two fantastic women, Nora Chahbazi and Celeste Hammell, who experienced reading difficulties within their own families and the schools they taught in. The foundation of their strategies have come from a variety of sources including research done by Diane McGuinness, a cognitive developmental psychologist of twenty five years and a professor at the University of South Florida. Diane has researched and published several books on reading. Both Nora and Celeste began their reading consulting careers with a program called Phono-Graphix. They trained hundreds of teachers in Phono-Graphix which lead them to delving deeper into effective and efficient reading strategies. The research they found and their own personal experiences resulted in the birth of Evidence Based Literacy Instruction (EBLI). The EBLI strategies are further supported by the data presented in *The National Reading Panel Report* published in 2000.

Besides compiling strategies that are firmly based on valid and reliable research, EBLI is streamlined. It teaches only what readers need to know to be proficient, not the seemingly endless "noise" in the form of extra rules, information, or tricks that are not necessary to teach reading. Teachers trained in these strategies learn to diagnose, prescribe, and get the student back on track in a short period of time (many times in only hours or weeks). In approximately 8 to 12 hours of one on one instruction, a struggling reader can increase two to four grade levels in reading. Those numbers do vary with each child but on average that is the length of time it takes. Even better is these results are reproducible and the strategies can be used with small or large groups at any age level. Anyone who has the desire and belief can learn how to use the strategies and get results. During trainings there are teachers, para-pros, parents, grandparents, and community volunteers in attendance. Everyone has one thing in common: the desire to teach kids to read and get them back on track quickly. In fact, it is probably easier for a non-teacher to learn the strategies because he/she does not have as much relearning and dumping of ineffective teaching tools that do not allow a student to reach their highest potential.

The goal and belief of teaching strategies that allow *all* students to reach their highest potential is another component that sets EBLI apart from other approaches. Because Evidence Based Literacy Instruction is founded on knowledge of how our language is put together, the most common spelling tendencies in the English language, and on how the brain organizes information, it allows *all* students to be the best readers they can be. In other words Evidence Based Reading Instruction works beautifully for all students and not just the struggling students. It does not teach strategies that only focus on achieving a specific grade level in reading or strategies that cannot be used past the third grade. It incorporates strategies *all* children can use from the very beginning of reading instruction and continue to use throughout a lifetime to reach their highest potential and become life long readers. The strategies that are taught allow *all* students to apply their skills in any and all text and at any grade level. The sky is the limit!

There are very few reading strategies or programs that approach the teaching of reading in this manner. The reasons that most reading programs fall short is they do not teach the logic of the English language nor do they teach consistently and systematically the knowledge that our writing system consists of approximately 44 phonemes (sounds) that are represented by letters.

EBLI also differs from the commonly used practices in today's schools by not teaching lists of words by sight. Students taught using the EBLI strategies do recognize the many "sight words" and eventually read them through memory because they have encountered them so often in text, although they are not initially taught as whole words. Many teachers across the nation, who teach lists of words as whole words, insist they cannot be "sounded out". For example the word "said". It is considered a sight word or "red word" because the spelling for /ĕ/ is spelled "ai". Educators have told children that you cannot sound out this word. But teachers who have knowledge of our English code say, "Yes you can!" The word consists of three sounds and you teach one of the spellings for /ĕ/ is "ai". Here are some examples of when a student would apply this knowledge: ag**ai**n, capt**ai**n, mount**ai**n, and porcel**ai**n. The teaching of whole words, intentionally or unintentionally, guides children into thinking that in order to read one must memorize words. This forces the student to use more working memory which decreases the amount of available working memory for the comprehension piece. In other words students are using much more brain power because they are trying to access thousands of pieces of information (words memorized) verses a few hundred (symbol to sound relationships and the spelling code) and applying them to the context. The teaching of sight words is unnecessary if students know the code of the English language.

The necessity of teaching efficient reading strategies is especially important because the ability to read has been linked to positive cognitive development. As Cunningham and Stanovich found in 1991," Those who read a lot will enhance their verbal intelligence; that is, reading will make them smarter." They found that "children who get out of the gate quickly-who crack the spelling to sound code early on- appear to enter into a positive feedback loop. One of the benefits of these reciprocation effects may be a level of participation in literacy activities that leads to a lifetime habit of reading and thus set the stage for future opportunities-opportunities not enjoyed by children who enter into this feedback loop more slowly." They also found that "High levels of decoding skill, is certainly a contributor to greater reading volume,... Good decoders read a lot and have the best context available for inferring new words." (Cunningham and Stanovich, 1998). This further supports the EBLI philosophy that educators cannot underestimate the value of teaching strategies which systematically and logically reflect the patterns within our alphabetic writing system when teaching reading so that *all* may reach their highest potential from the very start of reading instruction.

A third, common strategy used in today's schools that **is not** included in the E.B.L.I strategies is to look at the picture or the beginning sound of a word and "guess the word". This is absolutely an inefficient strategy at best and encourages guessing at words instead of accuracy in reading the words. This impedes comprehension and is obsolete in text with no pictures. Using this strategy really becomes pointless; once a student has knowledge of our language and knows the code they can read accurately and do not need pictures. *"Good readers read words with perfect or near perfect accuracy. The necessity of effective and efficient reading strategies*

*early on is imperative if we want all students to excel in academics."*
*(Chahbazi, 2004)*

Evidence Based Literacy Instruction strongly emphasizes accuracy. Students are able to be accurate readers. They do not have to guess because they have the knowledge of the English code that enables them to read accurately and efficiently. They are also taught a systematic method of decoding that increases fluency and comprehension.

# 8

# Nuts and Bolts

In Evidence Based Literacy Instruction, information, skills, and strategies are taught in a logical, sequential manner in order to improve reading comprehension and spelling. The strategies incorporate phonemic awareness which include, segmenting, blending, and phoneme manipulation that are necessary to manage the English code. Information about the symbols that represent each of the sounds in our language, the variety of spellings for each sound, and the overlap of various spellings are taught in a logical manner from simple to complex. These skills are necessary to read and spell words accurately, in the English language. Practice in guided oral reading (fluency), vocabulary, and comprehension are also a part of EBLI. This knowledge allows the student to reach their highest potential in reading and spelling. The student is then able to be immersed in vocabulary rich text that increases knowledge. The strategies are deeply immersed in instruction that incorporates the use of visual, auditory, and tactile to enhance learning and increase neurological pathways in the brain.

The process is fun and engaging. Students and teachers are able to explore and take notice of the amazing spelling patterns in the English language. Because EBLI uses a system of logic, it is not necessary to teach all of the spellings for all of the sounds in our language. The brain is able to systematically organize the information and add additional patterns (spellings) to the knowledge directly taught. Because the brain organizes information in patterns these common spelling tendencies are quickly stored in the brain for future use in reading and spelling. Many people trained in EBLI have said, "I will never look at a word the same again."

The EBLI strategies begin by teaching that the English language is made up of sounds. In order to access the sound you must be able to segment a word into its smallest phoneme or unit of sound. These sounds are then represented by symbols (letters) that are one, two, three, or four letters long. For example, the word *plant*; every sound in this word is represented by one letter. In the word *knot*; the spelling for /n/ is "kn". There are two letters representing one sound. In the word *light*, three letters represent one sound; "igh" is the spelling for /ī/. Lastly, in the word *though*, four letters represent one sound; "ough" is the spelling for /ō/. Once this is demonstrated, students are given opportunities to look at a variety of words, break them into their smallest units of sound, and study the spellings for different sounds. Usually a few sounds are signaled out to sort and discover the many different spellings.

One example of this is the sound /sh/. In the English language, there are approximately ten different spellings for /sh/. Look at these words and see for yourself:

fi**sh**

spe**ci**al

ini**ti**al

ma**ch**ine

**s**ure

mi**ssi**on

pen**si**on

ti**ss**ue

appre**ci**ate

an**xi**ous

These spellings are typically taught from the most common to the least common. This list reflects that order.

Another example of this is the vowel sound /oe/. In the English language there are seven different spellings for this sound.

b**oa**t

t**oe**

m**o**st

sl**ow**

d**ou**gh

s**ou**l

fl**oo**r

Again, these spellings would be taught from the most common to the least common. This list reflects that order.

While teaching common spelling tendencies in the English language, students are also taught that some of the same spellings represent more than one sound, for example the spelling "ea". This spelling can represent three different sounds in our language. Here are three examples: /ĕ/ as in br**ea**d, /ē/ as in m**ea**t, and /ā/ as in br**ea**k. After modeling this, students are given a variety of activities to discover for themselves other instances where the same spelling represents a different sound.

Segmenting and blending multi-syllable words is also modeled and practiced. Teaching a multi-syllable strategy that includes segmenting words into manageable unit's referred to as chunks or syllables, reading the unit, and then blending the syllables together yields accuracy during reading. This results in a decrease in the need for guessing and an increase in the student's fluency and comprehension. Fluency and comprehension are the next strategies (areas) to engage in with comprehension being the ultimate goal. This is accomplished with guided oral readings in authentic text and a variety of comprehension activities.

All of these strategies allow children to be actively engaged in their learning. After learning the strategies they now have a clear understanding of the alphabetic writing system and how to decode that system. As the student continues to grow and be immersed in more difficult text they are able to discover and easily connect other spelling patterns in the English language to previously learned information and steadily gain knowledge through text.

# 9

# How I Have Used EBLI

I've been lucky to have used Evidence Based Literacy Instruction in my classroom over the past five years. In those years, EBLI was used in small and large group settings with middle school students of all ability levels. These strategies have also been integrated into my 6th grade English curriculum with little difficulty. The strategies have helped all of my students be the best readers and spellers they can be. I also teach remedial reading classes for students who are two or more grade levels behind in reading. These students need a little more intense instruction and knowledge of the English code because until now they have never been able to see any pattern or system of logic within the English language. There are both regular education and special education students in my remedial classes.

In my 6th grade English classes, I teach the strategies very intentionally and systematically at the start of the year for approximately two weeks and integrate them into all content taught throughout the year. I have found that clear, systematic instruction on how our language is organized, knowledge of our alphabetic writing system, and the spelling tendencies in our language, along with daily practice in authentic text has dramatically increased fluency, spelling, and comprehension.

In my remedial reading classes, I am fortunate to have at least one, sometimes two teachers or para- pros instructing students with me. This added help enables us to set up centers or smaller groups within the class. These groups are involved in a variety of activities each day. Some of the activities are teacher driven and some are independent. The direct instruction groups practice learning different spelling patterns in the English language, decoding multi-syllable words, fluency, and comprehension while other independent groups are engaged in activities that enhance reading. For example, some students may be listening and following along with a book on tape, completing a computer assisted reading program that evaluates comprehension, or playing games that increase cognitive processing and/or visual motor skills, while others may be in the media center checking out books and reading silently. The centers vary according to the needs of my students. There are usually five centers set up in my classroom running each day. The students are put into groups of three or four. Each group will rotate to a different center each day of the week. This enables students to work with a teacher in a small group at least twice a week.

We have also established a system of documentation so that each time a group is with a teacher we know what has been practiced along with the strengths and weaknesses of each student. Along with this documentation the other teacher and I meet at least once a week to sit down and plan how each student is progressing along with any additional interventions they may need.

Several times a year we will complete a more formal analysis of how the student is doing. We always share this data with the student and the parents. In doing this we encourage the student to be more active in his or her own learning. It also gives the parent more information and understanding of what we are doing as well as why and how it is helping their child. By doing this there is more intrinsic motivation and students are constantly striving to achieve more. There is also more buy in and support from parents. Parents are more actively involved in their child's education and excited about the growth they see. As instructors, we use the data to track our teaching and to make sure that there is significant progress; if the student is not progressing, we change our approach.

When I say change our approach I mean that we have to take a closer look at the student to see where other weaknesses may lie. I am referring to an entire battery of knowledge and resources I have on cognitive development, perceptual development, neurological development, and speech and language development. I am, by no means claiming to be adept in all of these areas although I have learned how to complete some quick screenings and recognize deficits in these areas. With the help of experts who have a greater knowledge in these fields of study, I am *sometimes* able to confer and build a specialized program to help the student. Although, many times after conferencing with experts outside of the educational community I have found that some students must seek help outside of our school district in order for them to fill in the gaps that are missing. We (teachers) just do not have the depth and breadth of knowledge or time to successfully meet these children's individual needs.

Our teaching team's goal is to give the student strategies that will increase their reading comprehension and fluency in order for them to get back on track and out of our remedial program with the skills to excel at any and all levels of reading. When a student can decode words at the eleventh or twelfth grade level and can read 140-150 words per minute in grade appropriate text with comprehension, they are exited from our class.

The progress and amazing transformations that I have witnessed over the past five years have been inspirational! Children have gone from feeling inferior because they could not read or spell well, to being great readers and much improved spellers. I have also seen an increase in their writing skills and believe it is due to the fact that they are immersed in age appropriate text, have the ability to comprehend that text, and are more cognizant of the syntax within the English language. They have the skills and confidence needed to excel in their educational careers and beyond. They are able to choose their path with the tools necessary to be great readers. In fact, in five years of teaching these strategies to students with the most significant gaps in reading knowledge and who were participating in our special education programs due to a learning disability in reading; we have exited several students from special education and moved many others from special education English classes into general education English classes with no adjusted curriculum.

In the 2006-2007 school year, our Michigan Education Assessment Program (MEAP) tests also reflected our success. Each October in Michigan, students in grades 3-8 take a standardized test to monitor growth in reading, writing, and math. The assessment is designed to test the skills learned the year before. In other words the $3^{rd}$ grade test evaluates $2^{nd}$ grade skills, 4th tests $3^{rd}$ etc. After the first year, scores in our middle school ($6^{th}, 7^{th}$, and $8^{th}$ grade) improved dramatically(28%) and have continued to increase over the years. I make this statement because not only did our percentage of "proficient" students significantly increase in reading, but we continue to break a common trend across the state that has reflected scores at the middle school level to be dramatically lower compared to elementary scores. These scores are the result of our teachers searching for better ways to teach reading, learning new strategies, and implementing them. As of the fall of 2006, all of our teachers have been given a short training and classroom support in the EBLI strategies. They are currently using them in varying degrees within their content areas and in the reading classes they teach. After just one year of our entire staff focusing and intentionally using the strategies, we have also seen a dramatic increase in fluency and our English teachers have also witnessed significant increases in spelling accuracy.

# *10*

# Everyone Has a Story

Everyone has a story and each story is different. There is no doubt that being able to read fluently and comprehend opens doors to all of us and allows us to have more choices. By giving kids the gift of reading, they have been offered opportunities that were once not possible for them. As I tell all of my students, I want them to have the skills to do what they want and dream of doing. I don't want them to have to settle for a job they have to take because they cannot read. As stated earlier, increased ability to read leads to immersion in more text which as research has shown, leads to an increased in knowledge base.

By teaching kids to read accurately and fluently, we have also seen an increase in self esteem and a decrease in disruptive behaviors. I believe that these students now have the skills to prove to the world their intelligence! They are free! It's wonderful helping young people to believe again and witnessing them reach their highest potential!

Here are some amazing and joyful stories of triumph told to me by some of the parents of children with whom I have had the great pleasure of working with. The names in these stories have been changed for privacy purposes.

## Ben's Story

Ben was a tall and athletic eighth grade boy who came to us reading at the third grade level. He was diagnosed as learning disabled in reading and was in special education. We worked with him for two months. This is what his mother told me after two weeks of instruction:

Ben and his family were outside cleaning up the yard and they were yelling for Ben. He was on the four wheeler and they needed it. They kept calling and calling but Ben wouldn't answer. His mom went to look for him and found him just sitting on the machine staring at it. She asked him what he was doing and he said, "I'm reading these signs on the four wheeler. I could never read them before and didn't know what they said." Later his family was at Wal-mart and was once again trying to find Ben so they could get going. His mom found him standing in the front of the store looking up. She asked what he was doing and he said, "I'm reading the signs. I always wondered what they said." The last story she told was of a school night around 11:00 pm. She and her husband were getting ready to go to bed and noticed that Ben's light was still on in his bedroom. His dad went to check on Ben to see why he wasn't sleeping. Ben was reading one of his hunting magazines and just wanted to finish a good story.

## ___Andy's Story___

Andy was in 6<sup>th</sup> grade and in special education. His dad was very frustrated with our education system because he felt that we had failed Andy. When Andy came into our program he couldn't read above the 4<sup>th</sup> grade level. After being taught the EBLI strategies, his dad told me this story. One day they had gone to the store. After returning home everyone had gotten out of the family's mini van and was in the house. Andy had not come in the house and his dad assumed that Andy had stayed outside to play. After a while his dad looked out the window to see where he was. He saw Andy sitting in the van. He thought that Andy was just cleaning out the van. After an hour he looked out to see Andy still in the van. Andy's dad went out to check on him. He found Andy sitting in the van reading a book. He told his dad that he was at a really good part in the book and didn't want to stop. His dad told me that Andy is now an avid reader and always has his nose in a book at home.

## ___Jamie's Story___

Another story is about a young lady named Jamie. She came to us in summer school (August) reading below grade level and very, very slow. When she entered summer school she was using some very ineffective reading strategies. If she came to a word that she did not know she would have an entire dialogue about what that word might be. For example when she came to the word "splat" she had a conversation something like this:  It looks like the word "cat", but its not "cat" because it does not start with "c" and it can't be "bat" because it doesn't start with "b" ... This kind of strategy was very time consuming and by the time she figured out the word, she had forgotten what the context was about. By December she had increased her decoding and fluency by two years and was able to read more fluently at grade level. But what was the most inspiring to me was when I was sitting in church on Christmas Eve watching the children perform a short version of the story of Jesus' birth and Jamie was at the microphone reading. She was reading with confidence and fluency. What a wonderful Christmas gift! This particular young lady began working with us in August and her fluency was 25 words per minute accurately, in sixth grade text. By the end of the school year (June) she had increased to 120 words per minute, reading accurately in sixth grade text!

## *A Teacher's Son*

This story is about a fellow teacher's son, Will. I had worked with Will's mom for years and we had shared many stories about our kids. She had been worried since her son was in fourth grade about his lack of comprehension when reading and with his struggles to spell and write. She had spoken with me on numerous occasions about her concern that he could read very fluently, but could never remember what he had read. She had also said that he had a very hard time putting his thoughts down on paper and that his spelling was terrible. When he entered sixth grade she was worried because of the extra independent reading and writing he was required to do. One day her son requested to be in my remedial reading class. According to all of the testing data we had on him he wasn't a typical candidate for our class, meaning that his scores reflected that he was at grade level and on track with reading. But, he wanted to join. We worked with Will for three weeks and he was ready to be exited. A few weeks after we exited Will, he read an entire novel for the first time in his life and was able to tell his mom everything that had happened. His mom asked him what was different and what seemed to make the difference. He said, "I don't know but I can remember everything I read now." What was really fun was that his spelling also improved dramatically which gave him more confidence in writing. His writing became much more detailed after our class. Later, his mom confided in me that in the beginning she didn't really think that the strategies I taught would make that much of a difference, but they did. They gave Will the confidence to be an independent reader and learner. As time went on, she did not have to remind him to get his homework done nearly as much and she didn't have to read to him in order for him to comprehend the text.

## *What about Wyatt?*

Yes, what about Wyatt? This Wyatt would happen to be my 10 year old son who has also had his share of struggles with reading. And there are other kids that I have worked with who are very similar to Wyatt in that they did not learn how to read fluently in just 8-12 sessions of Evidence Based Literacy Instruction. Sometimes it may take a student a year or more to have everything click. There may also be other issues like visual or auditory processing, tracking of the eyes, memory, sequencing, simultaneous processing or language development that impedes the ability to read. These kids can and are helped although it takes more time, more practice, and a deeper knowledge about perceptual development, cognitive development, and multi sensory processing in order to correct these deficits.

My introduction to these scientific areas occurred when we first noticed that Wyatt had trouble with his letter formation in writing. Wyatt would form his letters from bottom to top and right to left. The problem with this was: in English, we read from top to bottom, left to right. This bad habit was slowing down Wyatt's fluency and making his writing difficult and sloppy. Another problem that Wyatt faced was he had learned how to read by memorizing words. For him, there was little connection between sound and symbols. There were chunks of information (words) and he memorized those words. He had very little decoding skills and consistently confused words like "who" and "how," "where" and "were" along with a variety of other word wall words that he had been taught to memorize. By the time he reached fourth grade his memory was maxed out. He did not have efficient skills to decode the increasing number of words, especially multi-syllable words. If he happened to come across a word that he had not memorized, he would just skip it or guess any word he already knew that looked visually similar. He was stuck somewhere at an early third grade reading level and was *ANGRY*.

We went to work teaching Wyatt the EBLI strategies and getting his writing on track. It was a very slow and laborious task. It was not easy for him to re-learn how to correctly form his letters.

It took him much longer to write because he had to think about the correct way to form the letter and then intentionally form them. His teachers tried to encourage him and check on him, but in a classroom with twenty five other students it was a challenge to say the least. His teachers did not understand nor use the EBLI strategies that Wyatt was being taught since they had not been exposed to these strategies. In other words, Wyatt was not being encouraged or guided to use the strategies in all subject areas and Wyatt, like many other children, wasn't going to try something new that was much harder for him, without consistent encouragement. Wyatt, being a typical kid took what he deemed to be the easier way out. Without the integration within his daily classes Wyatt reverted back to ineffective strategies of trying to memorize whole words and guessing. This led to a very frustrating year for Wyatt and his teacher. In order to cover up his inability to read at grade level Wyatt was the class clown, goofing off, and being off task before he admitted to anyone that he could not read. He also seemed to still exhibit some weaknesses in the areas of processing and sequencing. The year progressed and he managed to sneak though 4th grade and make it to summer vacation. Over the summer I worked with Wyatt on his reading using the Evidence Based Literacy Instruction strategies again. Wyatt was not overjoyed but did practice and improve his decoding to 5th grade and his fluency to 60 words accurately per minute in 5th grade text. He was still behind but he was much more hopeful that he could learn to read.

As Wyatt began 5th grade we had pretty much fixed the writing problem. For the first time in his educational career he was consistently forming his letters correctly. His "5" and letters "s, c, and p" were all going in the correct directions. However, he still struggled at times with "b and d". As the year began, I noticed many pages of notes in Wyatt's folders that were very sloppy and not complete. When I asked him about this, he just said that 5th grade was very hard and he couldn't write fast enough. I talked with his teachers and asked what they thought about his note taking. Many of them commented that Wyatt was very frustrated with taking notes from the board and many times did not finish. I immediately spoke with my friend Lynne Zimmer. She and I had both worked with Wyatt over that past two years and knew there was something else going on but we couldn't pin point it. She gave me the phone number of a pediatric occupational therapist (O.T.) that specialized in sensory motor integration. I spoke with her on the phone and she wanted to look at Wyatt to see if she could help. After meeting with the O.T., we found that Wyatt had tracking problems with his eyes. He was not physically able to track left to right without his eyes jumping around and losing focus. He was also not able to track from top to bottom. These two skills are imperative for Wyatt or any child to be successful in reading and copying from the board during class.

This awareness led to an entirely different realm of knowledge. I learned more and more about the many different tasks the eyes perform that are necessary for cognitive development. Before this experience I was only aware of visual acuity (seeing things clearly, 20/20 vision). I also learned about perceptual development and how humans take in information, process it, organize it into categories, and store it in long term memory. I learned about balance, timing, and crossing the midline of our body. All of these components allow us as human beings to gain knowledge. I also discovered there is a hierarchy of skills and if a student/human does not have these skills, they cannot perform at a higher cognitive level no matter how hard the teachers or student tries. Wyatt had some weaknesses in these areas and we needed to strengthen them. The good thing was that many of these areas were strengthened by "playing games". Fortunately, many of the activities Wyatt was involved in were physical and presented in a "game-like" format. He didn't mind going to the OT; he actually looked forward to going to the "fun lady's office". As of the writing of this book Wyatt has made huge gains in perceptual awareness, rhythm, balance, timing, sequencing, and processing. His teachers and I are starting to see the payoff of this practice within his daily academic activities. With these skills in place Wyatt's reading has also improved.

My point in sharing Wyatt's story is that using EBLI is absolutely an effective way to teach reading and will yield significant results, but not always within a few hours worth of work. There are always going to be those special cases that require more intervention. Besides reading interventions there may be other challenges such as having the student accurately practice and apply the skills in their daily activities. (It takes twenty one days to create a habit and six months to have it become automatic.) It may appear to the student that the old way was much easier. This, from their point of view, is accurate because they do not have to go back to relearn and undo strategies that are ineffective. It is hard for some to see and understand that in the long run the payoff of being a proficient reader and speller is immeasurable and will affect *all* aspects of their life

In Wyatt's case he is starting to see the benefits and understand the importance of it all, but there are many days when he still wants to do it the "old" way. I know that he will be just fine and we will get him through this "bump in the road" but I can't say it has been easy.

## *Emily's Story*

Since I have mentioned my other children in this book, it is only fair that I also tell Emily's story. Although I have to say Emily's is a much easier read. Emily is my middle child. She didn't really struggle with reading and kept pace academically with all of the grade level expectations. Although there is one area in which she failed miserably: spelling. As I worked with Hailey and Wyatt, Emily was frustrated because she wanted me to help her also. She knew that her spelling was awful which slowed her down when writing. What I knew was that her lack of knowledge of the English code was also slowing her down in the area of fluency. She was actually very good at the comprehension piece, she was just slow with the actual reading. In seventh grade her fluency was 120 words per minute in grade level text. After spending a few hours working with Emily using the EBLI strategies her fluency increased to 160 words per minute in eighth grade text. Her spelling also dramatically increased. And since her English teacher has learned the EBLI strategies and is integrating them into her spelling units, Emily's (and many other students) spelling accuracy has continued to increase. Since Emily now understands the logic of the English language she is able to reach her highest potential. She wasn't doing poorly without the knowledge. Her grades were all A's. The big difference is that now she has the knowledge to be a fantastic speller which will add to her writing abilities and when it comes to the ACT (or any other timed test) in high school, she will have the ability to get through all of the text. This will allow her to demonstrate her knowledge of content since she is now able to accurately and fluently read the test.

I have added Emily's story to the book for more reasons than just fairness to all of my children. I believe I am so very lucky to have the three very unique children I have because of what they have taught me. You see, if I had to group kids into three categories my children would represent each of these: 1) Children who have no understanding of the code (Hailey). 2) Children who have processing issues which impedes cognitive development (Wyatt). 3) Children who have been able to internalize enough of the code to excel in academics, but aren't working at their highest potential (Emily). ***All children benefit from Evidence Based Literacy Instruction.***

# *11*

# Lessons Learned

This is perhaps the most challenging section of the book for me to write. There is such an enormous amount of information that I have learned over the past four years. How to put it all down clearly and concisely? When stepping back and surveying the whole it seems that all of my learning can be summed up into 10 lessons:

*Lesson #1: Turn your anger into a passion.*

*Lesson #2: The lack of reading skills is a symptom not a condition.*

*Lesson #3: Think big and look for answers in new places.*

*Lesson #4: The need for engagement versus compliance.*

*Lesson #5: The need for quality remediation rather than accommodation.*

*Lesson # 6: Empowering students.*

*Lesson#7: Shift from grade level expectations to reaching ones highest potential.*

*Lesson # 8: Exchange excuses for answers.*

*Lesson #9: Separate self from the system.*

*Lesson #10: Change is the only constant in our universe.*

## *Lesson # 1 : Turn your anger into a passion.*

Personally, one of the most significant opportunities given to me throughout this process has been the chance to turn my anger into a passion. When this adventure began I was ***angry.*** Angry at myself for not being able to fix my child's reading problem. Angry at a system that was failing my child and many others. Angry with the politics embedded within the educational system that has nothing to do with what is best for children. Angry at other educators who didn't understand. Through the writing of this book I have learned that blaming others is useless and leads to many unnecessary battles. Where we are is simply where we are. We don't have to stay here and we certainly have an enormous amount of data and valid research to learn from in order to create something better. What is most important now is to share this knowledge and to have meaningful dialogue so that others can begin to question and learn. In doing this we may offer all children and teachers the opportunity to reach their highest potential.

## *Lesson #2: The lack of reading skills is a symptom not a condition.*

Academically, the most important thing learned is that the lack of reading fluency and comprehension is a symptom, not a condition. In most cases it is a symptom of not having the knowledge and understanding of how our language is organized, not knowing the code, and a lack of decoding skills. It may also be due to a lack of higher cognitive functioning skills like auditory or visual processing. Good teaching is like being a good physician.

Once teachers have a broader and more accurate knowledge of our language along with the most recent research on learning, the brain, and cognitive development; they are able to diagnose and prescribe—curing the illness. It is not impossible nor does it take years of remediation to fix a reading problem if a systematic, research based approach is used.

## Lesson #3: *Think big and look for answers in new places.*

When it comes to reading, many in the educational community do not integrate or in many cases have knowledge of the most recent and *scientific* data. It is clear that educators need more knowledge of what is happening in other fields that are connected to human development and learning. Many educators appear to stick with their "own kind"; meaning that they look mainly within the educational community for answers. This seems very unfortunate because there is so much to learn from other sciences. When it comes to reading there is a lot of theory being pushed. These ideas come with wide spread support, yet lack solid, long term evidence that they make a ***significant*** difference. Many strategies used in education over the past few years seemed like they *should* work, yet they yielded very little growth.

The scientific field approaches reading from a more scientific perspective which mandates solid data and proof. They are much more thorough with their research. They look through *years* of data. The information concerning reading published by the scientific community has given much more comprehensive knowledge.

This information allows educators to understand the whole child; enabling them to be diagnostic and prescriptive in teaching.

Barriers must be broken between the educational community and the scientific community. The knowledge from both schools of thought must be shared and integrated to create the best systems of reading instruction. There is so much knowledge to be gained when we all share our strengths and insights.

## *Lesson #4:    The need for engagement versus compliance.*

There is a difference between engagement and compliance, as was briefly mentioned in the preface. Our school systems, as they are currently organized, are based on a system of compliance. Compliance is defined in Webster's dictionary as: "1. a:  the act or process of complying to a desire, demand, or proposal or coercion. b:  conformity in fulfilling official requirements  2. a:  a disposition to yield to others"   In other words, compliance is doing what you are told. While Webster defines engagement as:  to hold attention of:  to induce to participate:  to take part. In other words being actively involved and committed to something. There is a big difference in these two principles and it does not mean that many teachers are not actively engaging students in their curriculum, although this knowledge gives all educators a lot to think about. Knowing and understanding the vast differences between these two ideas has forced me to take a good look at my teaching strategies and activities. Teaching reading using the EBLI strategies engages students which is another reason it produces such amazing results.

Students are engaged because there is a clear focus on the task and persistence with the task in spite of difficulties (in some cases children having to completely change their thinking of how the English language is put together). Students also continue to use the strategies even though there may be no extrinsic rewards.

## *Lesson #5: The need for quality remediation rather than accommodation.*

There is a difference between remediation and accommodation. In many schools across our nation teachers are taught to accommodate rather than remediate. The thought seems to be that at a certain point, if a child has not reached a specific reading competency level and educators have tried everything they know, the child is assumed to be "just wired differently" and will never be a strong reader. In other words, the child is unable to learn what is being taught for a variety of reasons and we must make accommodations. The accommodations include things like having someone read to the student or alter their assignments so they may learn content. The problem with this concept is that once we begin believing this, the student has no opportunities to improve his or her areas of weakness and this pattern will, more than likely, continue throughout their entire educational experience. Thus never pinpointing the areas of weakness and remediating them. This parallels the idea of injuring a body part and never engaging in physical therapy to rebuild that part. The thought that these children will always struggle to read or not be able read is simply unacceptable. If you look around any middle school across our nation many of these same students "with reading difficulties" have taught themselves an entirely new language in which they communicate (read and write) daily: instant messaging or text messaging. On their own, with no help from teachers, students have created their own language and effectively use it. This observation paints a pretty clear picture of the ability children have to read and comprehend if they are taught and engaged in a logical system.

Teachers do not participate in this cycle of accommodation to intentionally harm, but it is what we have been taught to believe. Although this paradigm is being challenged with ideas like "No Child Left Behind" which is trying to force our education system to reach all students and allow them to achieve at much higher levels. Yet there is still a flaw. The responsibility of correcting this problem is then put back on the teachers to come up with a way in which to teach the child so they may reach a set expectation. Unfortunately, teachers *have* tried everything they know and are usually not exposed to research in other non-traditional (non-educational) areas. They feel immense pressure to teach these children who in pervious years may have been labeled learning disabled or a slow learner and not expected to excel. Yet they are given no new strategies or tools to complete this lofty task. This is very frustrating and nearly a worthless endeavor unless there is a much larger amount of knowledge shared with teachers along with a complete restructuring of our educational system. What many in our government have not stopped to think about is that the *system* in which we have been trained in and are currently teaching within no longer serves our society. It does not and will not meet the needs or expectations of today's society. Much has changed since the 1920's. Today's society is so immensely different that it is almost as if we were on an entirely different planet. As Phillip Schlechty puts it in his *Creating Great Schools* book," Leaving no child behind is a noble sentiment, but ensuring that every child is empowered to get ahead is an even nobler goal."

## *Lesson # 6: Empowering students*

There is a part of remediation that has little to do with the distribution of knowledge. There is the part of building relationships, setting expectations, and believing in self. Students must be taught different strategies in order to reach their highest potential in reading, but they also must be given opportunities to engage in meaningful text, believe in themselves, and to know that they *can* read. This sometimes will take more time than teaching the strategies. Many of the students who end up in learning centers or remediation programs have had years of believing they cannot read along with reinforcement from external forces, like peers, and even their teachers to support that belief. One way to increase the student's confidence is for everyone to raise their expectations. Once a student has been taught the strategies immerse them in authentic text that is rich in vocabulary.

## *Lesson#7: Shift from grade level expectations to reaching ones highest potential.*

This next bit of information may explain why it is so challenging for some educators to change the way in which they teach reading.

The ideas of teaching children to reach "grade level expectations" and teaching children to reach their highest potential are two quite different philosophies. In reaching grade level expectations teachers are trained to have students accomplish a set of skills, which isn't a bad thing in itself. However, when it comes to reading in the lower elementary grades it gives teachers and parents a false sense of security. Many educators focus on teaching children lists of words which they can memorize and practice in regulated text, which leads to students appearing to be proficient in reading (scoring at grade level on many "tests"). Their main focus is on the test, which has been referred to as "teaching to the test". Although many of the students who are considered "proficient" at the early grades begin to fall behind in 4th, 5th or 6th grade and are unable to accurately read and comprehend authentic text as they progress. With the philosophy of teaching children so they may reach their highest potential, there is more emphasis on learning the building blocks of our language and creating a strong foundation so the strategies taught early on can be continually applied and refined in all reading situations at all grade levels.

## Lesson # 8: Exchange excuses for answers.

Another glitch educators face is when the teacher or school district is working very hard to reach those grade level expectations and the results from testing are not reflecting significant growth, some educators look for what I would call excuses instead of examining their methods. I have been just as guilty of this as any other teacher. It's an easy trap to fall into, especially if we believe that our training has been the most accurate and up to date. For years I believed, along with many others, that if a child couldn't learn how to read there must be something wrong with the child. After all, I had tried many different techniques, spent hours after school working with students, gone to trainings, and continued my education with more degrees. I was wrong. There were many areas of learning left unknown to me until my children guided me down other paths. This idea of excuses instead of answers became very clear to me one day as I engaged in a conversation with a local administrator. We were discussing the reading data from our MEAP testing and how I interpreted our middle school data as showing that EBLI has worked well and that it needed to be incorporated state and nation wide at the elementary level. This administrator made the statement that "we are right where we should be with our scores compared to our peer groups"; which meant that based on the socioeconomic grouping of our students we compared equally with other schools with the same demographics. As he continued to state how socioeconomics impacts our students and their abilities I immediately thought, since when did we strive and accept mediocrity? I realized that we each had much different expectations for our students. Because he knew how hard all of our teachers were working to increase reading comprehension and fluency within our district he was under the impression that we were doing *everything* possible to enhance student's reading. Although my experiences had shown me that there was much more to do and learn and with this added knowledge came the ability to teach so that every child could reach their highest potential. He expected many of our kids to struggle and not be high achievers because of their family income, which for me was and is *not* a factor in a child's ability to read at high levels. Our conversation also made me realize that we are right where everyone else is because everyone else is doing exactly what we are doing. Since then I have decided I don't want to be where everyone else is anymore and our kids don't want to be there either. Our students want and expect us to give them the knowledge that will enable them to achieve all goals they set for themselves.

## Lesson # 9: Separating self from the system.

In other words, who we are is not the system. We are separate, intelligent beings from the system in which we work. Just because the system is not working does not mean that we as educators are not working hard or are not intelligent. Separating ourselves from the system allows us to take an objective look at our accomplishments. Right now in America there are an estimated 40 million functionally illiterate adults. In our schools there are 40 – 60 percent of our students not performing "at grade level" in reading by the time they hit middle school. This is not because teachers, administrators, or students are lazy. This is because they are working in an outdated system with outdated tools. Instead of looking at the students who are not reaching their highest ability in reading as being "wired differently" or socio-economically disadvantaged, why don't we look at the way in which we teach reading and within the system which we work? Separating ourselves from the system will allow us to look at the system and make changes without feeling personally attacked. Think of it this way: If you had a physician that was only accurate in diagnosing your illness 50 – 60 percent of the time, would you continue to seek his professional opinion? Or if you had a bank that kept accurate track of your money only 60 percent of the time would you still bank there? And for all of you sports fans out there, if your favorite professional sports team only won 40-50 percent of its games year after year would that coach still be leading the team?

Our nation, our society, and many educators are demanding that all students reach their highest potential in reading. We can meet that demand but only with a big shift in the educational system of the United States, our thinking, and enhanced knowledge.

## *Lesson #10: Change is the only constant.*

Change is one of the only constants in our lives. Everything is always changing. In other words a person is either changing or disintegrating. You can take the opportunity to learn and grow or not. The choice is yours.

# 12

# No Child or Teacher Left Behind

With the No Child Left Behind (NCLB) legislation it is clear that our nation has taken notice of the huge deficit in many children's learning especially when it comes to reading. In an effort to reduce the gaps and allow all children to reach their highest potential NCLB was enacted. Schools are now required to annually assess student's progress and document what is being done to bring up the scores of those students who have not met the standard criteria. This is all good, although teachers and our K-12 public education schools are left with a big job. For most it is like trying to produce a corvette using technology of Henry Ford and his model T.

There has been a mandate to have all children achieve higher standards in reading, which I support and am a firm believer in. Although the tools, ideas, and programs that are being used to achieve this goal are still stuck in a system that was designed to only allow a small number to reach their highest potential. K-12 schools across the nation are scrambling to find better strategies and programs that will produce higher test scores, but do they truly believe that *all* children can read at much higher levels? Nearly all of the programs being peddled are still immersed in the idea that not all children will learn how to read. Many programs are just the same techniques used over the past twenty years, with a different name or cover. Why? It sells. It is within everyone's comfort zones.

What are our colleges and universities doing with their teacher training programs? Has there been a paradigm shift? Has there been open communication between the cognitive sciences and education departments so that teachers are trained using the most up to date, scientific data on reading instruction, the human brain, perceptual development, speech and language development, and how all of this is connected? If there is not a shift at the college and university level these institutions will continue training teachers for a system that is crumbling and schools that no longer exist. The educational system cannot remain as it has for decades and meet the demands of today's global society.

No Child Left Behind has left K-12 teachers holding the bag. Teachers are given the burden to bridge the gaps and fix children while using outdated training methods that have no intention of allowing all children to reach their highest potential. It has been accepted by society, up until recently, to have 40-50 percent of our student population academically successful while the rest struggled or dropped out. Now society and our global economy are demanding more from our schools, which is good for our children and nation. It's just the programs and ideas that are deeply entrenched in the system do not support this shift. As said earlier, we are trying to build a corvette using the same technology and methods that Henry Ford had while building his Model-T.

Here is an example. This is an actual situation encountered in my classroom last year. This is the story of a sixth grade student who we'll call Jane. Jane had struggled in school for years. She struggled mainly with reading. She received reading instruction using the EBLI strategies and improved greatly in her ability to read and comprehend, although she was still lagging behind her classmates in comprehension and fluency. When she entered my classroom she was eleven years old. As I worked with her I noticed she was rubbing her eyes a lot and often complained of headaches while in reading class. On a hunch I did a quick check of her visual motor skills. What I found was very surprising. I had her follow a pencil toward her nose and away from her nose which checked for convergence. I found that Jane's left eye was unable to follow. Both of her eyes were able to track my pencil toward her nose until the pencil was approximately 12-15 inches out. At that point Jane's right eye continued to track while her left eye simply stared straight ahead. No wonder she had headaches and her fluency was still slow. Her eyes were not working together at about 12 inches out which is where she would hold all text in order to read it. Think about the impact that has on reading. As she would try to read anything only one eye was tracking. After school I showed her mother what had been discovered and explained what kind of a problem that led to with reading. Her mother could not believe it. There were some indications that there also may have been other motor skill problems with the left side of her body. Her mother confirmed that she was born premature and when she ran the left side of her body did not work like her right side. Not being a physical therapist or medical doctor, I could not fix those deficits although it's not hard to realize that if her left side were not able to function correctly it impeded her ability to learn many things. Now what to do? Who was equipped to evaluate and remediate this young lady in order for her to reach her highest potential? I certainly didn't have the knowledge or training. The only reason I knew the little I did was because my son had previously had some visual motor processing problems and I had learned a little from the physical therapist I'd taken him to. Some of my peers knew what I was talking about, but none had any knowledge of how to fix this problem. Many did not really understand how this connected with teaching reading or learning.

How does this connect to NCLB? Here was a student with visual motor processing problems along with possibly other processing problems. I had not been trained in any of the knowledge needed to fix this problem, yet I was responsible to get her to grade level and beyond in reading. No matter how hard she and I tried we were going to make very little progress unless this visual motor processing was addressed. The best that could be done within the system was to have our intermediate school district occupational therapist (OT) evaluate and work with her. The problem was that our OT was assigned to three different school districts and responsible for many other children throughout our intermediate school district. When I contacted our occupational therapist and described what had occurred she was very surprised. Her comment to me was, "I usually don't have conversations like this with teachers. How do you know about this?" She was right. Teachers are not given this kind of information in their education courses. Our OT was able to work with Jane for a few weeks and improve her convergence. Jane is doing much better and she does not have the headaches although there is more to uncover with her. I feel all we gave Jane was a "band aid". Our OT did not have the time to pursue other issues that were impeding Jane's motor skills and processing. These things needed to be addressed in order for Jane to reach her highest potential in reading and to have continued success in school. Jane is not the only child I have encountered with visual motor problems.

Another student I had could not track with his eyes from top to bottom. As he would follow my pencil from above his head to below his chin his eyes would jump up and down. He was not conscious of his eyes doing this but it did significantly impede his ability to take notes from the board to his paper. Who was going to work with him and train his eyes and when? Another student I had was unable to track from left to right. Her eyes would jump or quiver as she crossed the midline of her body. She complained of losing her place while reading. These problems were impeding the students' fluency and comprehension. How were these to be fixed and when?

These are some problems that teachers who have a little additional knowledge and training face. While other teachers have no knowledge of perceptual development, visual or audio motor processing skills, etc. and how they must be in place for higher order learning.

Our schools need to be reconstructed. Each school needs to function more like a hospital in which everyone is given the most up to date, research based information of how to teach, while others specialize in specific areas. When there is a problem diagnosed, a prescriptive treatment must be implemented to bring the child up to speed effectively and efficiently. This will require both the educational community and medical community to join forces and share their knowledge in order to allow all children to reach their highest potential and to build a strong nation.

No Child Left Behind has brought to light an illness that must be cured in our nation, yet it has not addressed the more serious problem of restructuring an outdated system and retraining those that work within this system.

# 13

# Why Me?

There are days when I gaze at the faces of the children in my remediation class and feel as if I am running a trauma unit where slowly, piece by piece, children are being put back together after they have been torn apart by our educational system. With the information and data that is available today there is no reason any child with an IQ of 70 or better should be labeled learning disabled in reading. Some of these children have been told they can't read and will never be good readers. While others have simply drawn this conclusion after years of pullout programs or special reading interventions that haven't worked. Their scars run deep.

Those are the days I ask, "Why me?" Why do I get to be the one who has asked the questions, lived through the pain of my daughter's suffering, and been ostracized by some of my cohorts in education? Why me?

If I had a dollar for every time I thought or asked that question I could probably afford a quiet little retirement home on a desolate section of beach somewhere. I could live there quietly without stirring up controversy…maybe.

I do not have the answer to that question nor do I care anymore. Every step of this journey has led me to an awakening; a deeper understanding of who I am and what can be done. I do not work for my principal, my superintendent, or the school board. I work for the children; each child that enters my classroom and others throughout this country who are suffering from the inability to read proficiently. *Every* person whom I have encountered on this path (both supportive and non-supportive) has assisted me in finding answers, clarifying goals, and sharing knowledge. I am not any more important than anyone else on this path. Nor am I more important than anyone who has yet to begin asking questions. We all have our jobs to do in eradicating illiteracy. Each job has equal importance. We cannot help our children unless everyone uses their strengths and gifts to do what they can. By coming together and sharing, we create something so powerful, so amazing, that no task is too large. I know this is possible because of the many incredible experiences and people I have come to know and communicate with throughout this journey.

Some may call me naive or a dreamer. I prefer to call myself a catalyst. According to Webster, a catalyst is "1: a substance that initiates a chemical reaction and enables it to proceed under different conditions than otherwise possible. 2: one that provokes significant change."(Merriam-Webster 1984) My job is to get people thinking, searching, and sharing: To help others understand they are not alone and let them know that it is ok to be honest with themselves. By questioning, learning, and discarding misinformation educators will be able to make room and assimilate new information. We can acquire knowledge and skills that will allow us to go beyond that in which we are accustom and experience many new joys.

# *14*

# **What's Your BS?**

**O**ur BS is our belief system. Our belief system determines how we think, how we interact or react, and our perceptions. To put it quite simply, the only thing preventing anyone from learning or experiencing anything new is their BS. Our BS allows or disallows us to embark upon a variety of experiences. Our belief system is that which we believe to be true, what we base all of our decisions on, and how we interact with our life experiences. Our BS is the accumulation of thoughts and ideas each of us have gathered over a lifetime through what we have seen, heard, experienced or been taught. Sometimes our BS is so strong it wraps us in a blanket and does not allow us to have new experiences. We are sure that we "know the outcome" so we do not engage in the new experience. Belief systems can change and do change all of the time. All it takes is a little courage and some curiosity. It happens when we humans start asking questions like: "What if…?", "How come…?", and "Why not…?" This questioning opens us up just enough to let some new experiences or knowledge flow to us.

Think back to when you were a child. Think of some of your most vivid memories and experiences. Many of those memories are of activities or events that you didn't want to try. Maybe these experiences pushed you out of your comfort zones or elements. Some of those memories or experiences may have turned out just as you expected, while many others did not. Those unexpected outcomes led to a changing of your BS.

The good thing about belief systems is they ***can*** change. When we as humans change our belief system it opens up opportunities for new and exciting experiences and possibilities. If we do not take the opportunity to question our BS then we will be forever in the same pattern; having the same experiences with the same results. Benjamin Franklin once said, "The definition of insanity is doing the same thing over and over and expecting to get different results."

If educators want to increase our children's ability to read, if our society and nation has changed its expectations about the number of children who need to be competent readers; we must change our BS. We must look at some of the most recent and comprehensive data available about our language, reading, reading instruction, the human brain, and learning and change our belief systems. We must step out of our comfort zones and stretch ourselves, mentally, physically, and emotionally. It can be done. People are doing it everyday. There is so much more to learn and do in order for us to create an educational system in which everyone can reach their highest potential.

It is kind of humorous, yet sad when I see news headlines about this athlete or another breaking a record that was thought to be "impossible" or scientists doing "the impossible". Why can't teachers do things that are thought to be "impossible"? All of the great leaders, thinkers, and inventors throughout history have changed their BS and done what was once thought impossible.

Teaching reading so that all children can learn to read, write, and spell at much higher levels was once thought to be impossible. That is no longer true. There is *no* reason that any child in the United States of America should be labeled learning disabled in reading or writing ever again.

# 15

# Where Do We Go From Here?

Where do we go from here? Good question. If any of us are going to elicit any change we must first look within ourselves. The starting point with all of this is to look at our own ideas, philosophies, concepts, and begin to ask why we have them. It will take a little bit of digging because, if you are like me and many other humans, you will first be angry and want to place blame somewhere besides yourself. Keep digging; be aware of your ego and how it plays a big part in all of this. It does *not* serve you well.

When this adventure began I was depressed and felt powerless. As I learned more I then became angry. I was angry at the system, angry at people because they did not understand or didn't want to change, and angry at the time wasted trying to learn things that were not worthwhile. The truth is that without all of these experiences I would have never kept searching for answers. As one resistance led to another, I was given the opportunity to keep searching and to keep questioning. I had the opportunity to change my belief system. I tried to keep moving forward and leave the past in the past, live for the moment and the future, although I would many times think back and get angry at people and events. Eventually after I peeled away all of the layers and let go of old concepts; I realized there was a way to teach *all* children to read. These strategies were supported by the most recent scientific data, not theory. They were not difficult to implement although it took a lot of relearning and training. This led me to an awakening: a need to guide as many as I possible to this new awareness and knowledge. I wanted to help my own children, my students, my staff, my school system, and now the nation. In doing this my goal is to create a system that allows all to reach their highest potential.

It is challenging to stop and truly evaluate ourselves and the systems in which we have so strongly identified with. There are many difficult challenges that we face and none of us will have the same experience; although the outcome will be the same. This adventure will lead you to your highest purpose and allow you to be who you truly are, an amazing and highly intelligent human being that can help others reach their highest potential.

For whatever reason, you have this book in your hands. And if you have read this far you must have some interest in learning about reading. You now have the opportunity to make a choice; decide what you are going to do with the information that has been presented. Do you choose to support a system that does not and cannot in its current state allow all to reach their highest potential? Or do you choose to gain new knowledge, search a little more?

I have tried to be painfully honest and tell my story so that others may learn and have an easier path. We can all begin the tidal wave of change by doing what we can. Not forcing others or engaging in conflict but educating; doing what we do best, teaching and learning.

Whether you are a parent, a teacher, administrator, or interested community member; start asking questions. Look at how your students are performing. Are they reaching their highest potential? Do you believe that all students can perform at much higher reading, writing, and spelling levels? Do you believe that in this amazing world we live there may be more answers worth searching for?

# Epilogue

As I look back over the past few years and the evolution of this book I realize that the title not only describes my daughter and her experiences, but mine as well. I was learning disabled in many ways as this journey began. I was disabled by a system that wanted to keep me in a little box, controlled by others. I was disabled by my own ego, arrogance, and ignorance; thinking that I knew all there was to know about reading or wanting to blame others for the problems I encountered. By asking questions, searching for answers in a variety of places, and accepting responsibility for my actions I have been enabled. I have been enabled to learn new things and speak honestly, lovingly, and openly about subjects many are afraid to talk about. It has been an amazing journey with much enlightenment. It's a journey that will never end, as I continue to learn more everyday. At times, this journey has not been easy, but I am glad I have stayed the course. This adventure has allowed me to free myself and reach for my highest potential. I hope that in telling my story it will give others courage to reach their highest potential. The best advice that I can give at this point is *to question everything and to follow your heart.* These two things will guide all of us to our highest potential.

Love and peace to all who have read this book.

# About the Author

Wendy Crick has been teaching English at the middle school level for the past twenty years. Her thirst for more knowledge about reading instruction, how humans learn, and creating a better system of teaching reading in public schools has been a driving force in her life for the past ten years. She lives in Northern Michigan with her husband and three children. She also shares her life with four horses, two donkeys, two cats and two dogs. She enjoys learning and adventure and has very few days without both.

# Bibliography

Chahbazi, Nora and Hammel, Celeste. "Evidence Based Literacy Instruction", training seminar, Ounce of Prevention Reading Center, Flushing, Michigan. 2007.

Cunningham, Anne E. and Stanovick, Keith E. "What Reading Does For The Mind." *American Educator* Washington DC., 1998.

Denninson, Paul E. and Gail E. *Brain Gym.* Ventura, California: Edu-Kinesthetics, Inc. 1998.

Flesch, Rudolf. *Why Johnny Can't Read and What You Can Do About It.* New York, NY: Harper & Row Publications Inc. 1986.

Kranowitz, Carol Stock. *The Goodenoughs Get in Sync.* Las Vegas, NV:Sensory Resources LLC., 2004.

Kranowitz, Carol Stock. *The-Out-of-Sync Child.* New York, New York: Penguin Group 2005.

Kranowitz, Carol Stock. *The Out-of-Sync Child Has Fun.* New York, New York, Penguin Group, 2003.

Leman, Nicholas. "Reading Wars." *Atlantic Monthly* November 1997, vol. 280, p. 128-134.

Lewin, Tamara. "The Scope of the Issue." *New York Times* March 17, 1996.

Lyn, Reid G. et al. *America Reads Challenge.* National Institute of Child Health and Human Development (NICHD) Research.

McGuinness, Diane. *Early Reading Instruction: What Science Really Tells Us About How to Teach Reading.* Cambridge, MA: MIT Press, 2004.

McGuiness, Diane. *Why Our Children Can't Read.* New York: Simon and Schuster/Free Press 1997.

Monaghan, E. Jennifer. "Phonics and Whole Word/Whole Language Controversies, 1948-1998: An Introductory History". 1998.

Peterson Directed Handwriting, "Information Directory" March, 2008,

Rosner, Jerome. *Helping Children Overcome Learning Difficulties: A Step-By-Step Guide for Parents and Teachers.* New York: Walker Publishing Company 1979.

Schlechty, Phillip C. *Creating Great Schools: Six Critical Systems at the Heart of Educational Innovation*. San Francisco, CA: Jossey-Bass 2005.

"Summary of the (U.S.) National Reading Panel Report: Teaching Children to Read". Newark, DE: International Reading Association 2002.

Zimmer, Lynne. Learning Solutions Inc. Harbor Springs, Michigan 2007.